BOOST

Powerful tools to Re-energize and Re-engage You and Your Team in Crazy Times

Also by the author

Shift or Get Off the Pot

BOOST

POWERFUL TOOLS TO RE-ENERGIZE AND RE-ENGAGE
YOU AND YOUR TEAM IN CRAZY TIMES

LINDA EDGECOMBE

INSOMNIAC PRESS

Library and Archives Canada Cataloguing in Publication

Edgecombe, Linda, 1960-
        Boost! : re-energize and re-engage you and your team in crazy times / Linda Edgecombe.

ISBN 978-1-897415-27-6

1. Teams in the workplace. 2. Employee motivation. 3. Organizational effectiveness. I. Title.

HD66.E34 2010   658.4'022   C2010-904610-2

The publisher gratefully acknowledges the support of the Department of Canadian Heritage through the Book Publishing Industry Development Program.

Printed and bound in Canada

Insomniac Press
520 Princess Avenue,
London, Ontario, Canada, N6B 2B8
www.insomniacpress.com

Canada

CONTENTS

Introduction

Do you need to give you and your organization an energy boost? What do you need to help you re-focus, re-energize, and re-invent how you and your team see life and work? Do you want to:

- Increase efficiency and creativity?
- Increase endurance, with energy to spare?
- Feel revitalized and positive?
- Have an emotional connection to your work and your family?
- Be driven to be outstanding in your field?

Then read on!

How do you know if you need this book? Let's take a look at two crucial tools for determining your level of need: 1) The Engagement Audit, and 2) The Energy Quiz.

The Engagement Audit

1. **Energy.** Do you feel energized in all aspects of your life, including physical, emotional, mental, and spiritual?

2. **Connectedness.** Do you have a sense of belonging within various organizations, groups, and teams? This means both in and out of work. How connected do you feel?

3. **Character traits.** What areas of your life are working well for you? Are you aware of your communication style and what people hear when you speak to them?

4. **Trust.** This is, of course, the basis of every team; whether it's at home or at work. It's the characteristic you need to dip into to maintain full engagement at all times.

5. **Awareness.** How aware are you while dealing with tough issues that arise? For instance, are you aware when your team's buttons get pushed?

6. **Perspective shifting.** This is a skill that takes practice and becomes the best coping mechanism we can draw on. How judgemental are you? Can you catch yourself when your judgements begin to surface?

7. **Contribution.** Do you currently give back somewhere in some manner that is not about you?

The Energy Quiz

1. **I find it difficult to take time out to exercise.**
   True   Sometimes True   Not True

2. **I often skip meals—especially breakfast—or go for long periods without putting food in my mouth.**
   True   Sometimes True   Not True

3. **I never get enough sleep.**
   True   Sometimes True   Not True

4. **The amount of water I drink a day is:**
   0–2 glasses   2–5 glasses   5–9 glasses

5. **I am a worrier and have many thoughts running through my head as I try to fall asleep.**
   True   Sometimes True   Not True

6. **I have no idea how balanced my diet is on any given day.**
   True   Sometimes True   Not True

7. **I often grab a quick lunch at a fast-food restaurant.**
   True   Sometimes True   Not True

8. **I'm an all-or-nothing kind of person: either I'm eating healthful meals and working out every day or I'm pigging out and acting like a couch potato.**
   True   Sometimes True   Not True

9. **I don't keep a food and exercise journal.**
   True   Sometimes True   Not True

10. **I haven't laughed so hard it hurt within the last month.**
    True   Sometimes True   Not True

11. **I can't remember the last time I was by myself in quiet contemplation.**
    True   Sometimes True   Not True

The bottom line is that if you answered "true" or "sometimes true" to more than four of these questions, you are probably energizing yourself with caffeine and/or adrenaline. Among the things I cover in this book are simple steps for getting your energy back and helping you feel more engaged in your work and home life.

The Plan

This seven-step plan to improve both your energy and engagement will be the best detox your work team or family has ever experienced. I know, for many of you, that the idea of a detox causes you to clench your behinds. However, fear not: this detox will have you and your team skipping to work and back home again. It will require buy-in from everyone concerned, and in some cases, it will be necessary to give tough love to those who will be the *energy administrators* of this challenge.

So re-energizing and engaging your team is something you need to act on. In a snapshot, energy is a physics equation. What you put out is directly related to what you get back in return. It is just simple science. The following seven challenges may be completed in whatever order you wish. Some will be easier than others, and some will be downright challenging, but persevere.

As the *energy catalyst,* you will have to get full support and buy-in from your team before setting out on the challenge. Don't worry though; even if you only get a few of the following challenges completed, you will have started the proverbial energy ball rolling and you will see a change in you and your team. The most important goal is to have fun while you do it, or don't even bother starting. Let me say that one more time: have fun.

Now just get started.

Before You Start the Book—Check Your Judgements at the Door

Here's the short story on judgements. We all make them, all the time, if not most of the time; we are not even aware that we are doing it. It's our ego's way of staying strong. And, for some bizarre reason, we think we feel better when we judge others. So all I am going to recommend here is, for the sake of your own energy, just *notice* when you are making judgements. Now, I realize that this will take some practice on your part. You will find that your judgements are relentless, but try this for just a day to start, and when you catch yourself judging someone, or something else, just observe yourself doing it. By doing so, you will create a space between your subconscious mind and who you really are. You will find yourself more in the moment and your judgements will be "checked at the door."

One last thought before you start. I have always had the thought that every book, both fiction and non-fiction, needs one good love story with a steamy scene about three quarters of the way through to help you, the reader, get through it. So I thought I would start that trend with this book. How steamy, you ask? Well, let's just say it's steamy enough to get you three quarters of the way though and you can then make up your own mind. I mean, come on, I did use the word *crazy* in the title, so I had to add a bit of crazy into the content. And besides, a good love session is not only engaging, it's very energizing, so quite fitting in this book, I do believe.

Three Quarters of the Way to Love

For many months, Tessa and Jake had been lusting for each other. They actually were in love but weren't quite aware that's what it was just yet. You see, they met on the subway on their way to the same co-op job interview several months earlier. Both were attending Berkley, taking a business internship program, and each was trying to land a great job that would both pay for the massive student loans they had accumulated and kick-start their lives. It was time for both to step into the "real world"—the world that comes with a desk, a title, an inbox, an outbox, and a decent paycheque every month to pay for the life they knew they wanted but just hadn't identified yet. So on this very busy Thursday, during a staff meeting, Tessa sent Jake a quick text, wondering if he wanted to possibly meet for a drink after work today. Why a text? Well, you see, no one in the office knew about their mutual attraction yet. Heck, even they hardly knew....

Their boss, John, had just returned from a strategic leadership convention and was eager to share with them the latest and greatest team enhancement activity that would make them all more productive and happier at work. So before Jake could respond to Tessa's text with his reply, John asked everyone in the boardroom to put all cell phones, laptops, and PDAs in the basket that he was sending around the room.

"Yes everyone, we are going old school for this meeting and maybe even longer."

With great hesitation, everyone put their phones and laptops into the basket.

"I know it seems odd," John added, "but we are going to get through one meeting without phones going off,

buzzing. None of us will surf the Net and read e-mails on our computers while we discuss what's happening for each of us at work right now.

Now Tessa's ticked off. She just wanted a simple yes, and so she begins her latest skill of reading body language, hoping Jake knows how to signal a yes with his body. Oh boy, was this going to be one odd meeting!

Chapter One

TECHNOLOGY: LOVE IT AND SOMETIMES LEAVE IT—
DISCONNECT TO RE-ENGAGE

Here is the challenge you must take on and it won't be easy. How's that for a sales pitch? The truth is, this step will be difficult for most people. So let's start out with a simple task. Choose a day, and I will suggest a Friday, that everyone on your team goes for an entire day without cell phones, pagers, BlackBerrys, iPhones. This is for your team at work, but it could also include your family team. It means no text messaging, TV, video games, computers, radios, CD players, any of it. You must have face-to-face conversations and simply amuse yourselves by being with the people on your team or in your family.

At the end of this day, journal a bit about how the day went for all of you and then set some time to share this experience with one another. Yes, the withdrawal may cause some headaches. Just make a cup and tea and you will be all right.

I recently flew home from Toronto to Kelowna, which is a four-hour flight. Just before we boarded, the woman at the gate announced that all the TVs on the plane were not working, so she suggested that we quickly go and buy a magazine.

I had my iPod Touch, but when I checked it, I found it to be completely dead. There was no battery power at all, and I did not have my computer charger to quickly boost it. Once on the plane, the flight attendant Brad made a joke and told us that we might have to amuse ourselves by actually talking to each other. *Ahh!* That's not what I do, I thought, I speak for a living and didn't want to do any more of it today. But, as a consolation, Brad told us that he would be running some games on the plane a couple of times over the next four hours. Yay, I thought. And it just so happened that I was sitting beside a very chatty young man who tended to talk a bit too loud for my liking, but he was pretty funny.

Brad started up his first game an hour into the flight. "Name the Baby," he called it. Well, wouldn't you know it, the plane was all abuzz. He gave out prizes and we all had a good laugh.

Brad fired up his second game two and a half hours in, which he called "The Toilet Paper Race." He pitted both sides of the plane against each another, left side of the plane versus the right side. Now we were all fired up. It felt like I was on the bus of one of those university ski trips. Well, okay, minus the kegs of beer. Four hours went by so fast, and the energy on that bus—I mean *plane*—was awesome! So no phones, no BlackBerrys, no computers, no movies, and, yes, I can report that we all survived. Not only that—it was a blast!

Disconnect To Re-Engage and Just Notice What You Notice

Okay, businesspeople of the world, put down your cell phones, BlackBerrys, PDAs, Pocket PCs—whatever—and *focus*. This may sound amusing, but I'm dead serious. Oh, and I don't mean turn them to vibrate, stun, or whatever setting you normally do to appear courteous. I want you to *shut them off*. Off means *off!* But, wait, there's more: I want you to keep them off for one full day.

Are you addicted to your communication devices? It seems that many of us are, and after thousands of car accidents and several deaths later, legislators have stepped in to take them away from us. Yes, it is becoming law in many provinces and states that the use of handheld devices in vehicles is now illegal. Even Oprah Winfrey is begging us to make our cars a "no phone zone."

Earlier this year, Oprah featured Peter Walsh on one of her episodes. He put out a challenge even bigger than my one-day challenge. So for those of you who really want to re-connect your families, homes, colleagues, and workplaces, take the "Disconnect to Re-Engage" Challenge. WARNING: You will feel naked, so bring a small blanket with you for the day, just so you have some security as you try and navigate through the quiet and calm.

Are You Hooked on Electronics?

A recent poll taken by Ipsos-Reid showed that across North America

- 92% of knowledge workers (folks who use a computer at work) read, send, make, or take work-related communications during non-work situations;
- 73% keep their work communication devices on over the weekend;
- 45% still tune into the office while on vacation;
- More than half of the working population (55%) communicate about work in social situations, including while spending time with their families, over dinner, and on dates, while about 20% have cut a date short to take a work call or respond to a work message;

- 6% of the population always ignore the request to turn off phones and PDAs while in meetings, church, plays, and movie theatres;
- 12% have responded to a call, text, or e-mail while making love to their partner.

Okay, I made the last one up; I just wanted to see if you were still paying attention. But I'll bet some of you have done this too!

Before you look at the effects of this obsessive behaviour, which we tend to continue to condone, we need to ask ourselves why we keep doing it and what's the payoff? Cell phones had their first surge in popularity back in the early '90s, and by 1995 cell phone sales in North America exceeded the birth rate, according to the CIA World Factbook, and as of 2008, there are 270 million cell phones in the U.S. and 21.5 million in Canada.

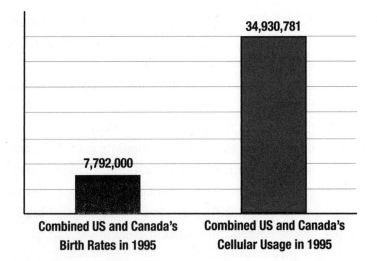

Combined US and Canada's Birth Rates in 1995 — 7,792,000

Combined US and Canada's Cellular Usage in 1995 — 34,930,781

Have we whittled down our ability to connect face to face with people and replaced the skill of conversation with our current version of *virtual relationships?*

How to Tell If You Need This Challenge
Signs you need a detox—on a cellular level:

1. If you have checked for messages in the past ten minutes, you need to detox.
2. If you have ever scrolled e-mails over the dinner table, you need to detox.
3. If you have checked messages while on vacation, right after (or during) lovemaking, and/or while the kids opened their Christmas or birthday gifts, you need to detox.
4. If you have checked messages during your weekly visit to church, synagogue, mosque, or your in-laws, you need to detox.
5. Okay, simply if you own a cellular device, you need to detox.

I know using these electronics is safe. You can think before you type, and we all feel very self-important; you know, that "I'm needed" feeling you get when your little personal excitement device vibrates on your hip. I can feel the wall of reasons that are coming up why *you* are different from the other billion businesspeople on the planet who are also addicted to their connection crutches, but to tell you the truth, you are not. I'm sorry to break that news to you.

Those Who May Be Exempt

If you are actively working in an emergency room, are an "on call" doctor or EMT, or even if you are currently on call as an emergency service repair technician, then you can keep yours on during the times you are on call. Heck, I will venture a bet that even the President of the United States turns off his "find me anywhere" personal pocket locator to have dinner with his family or tuck in his kids for bed.

For the rest of you who are saying to yourselves, "What if…someone really needs me?" or better, "I make my living in sales with my cell phone" (that includes you realtors), well tell your clients and colleagues up front to call you on your land line and *leave a message* if you don't answer. This challenge is only for a day. Come on, people!

What's the Upside?

Now here's a novel thought about what you can do with all that extra time you will have on your hands this day: go and buy yourself a stamp, and then put pen to paper and write someone a letter. You may need a massage afterwards to help with the cramps you will experience, but whomever you write to will love receiving your letter later that week.

The real reason you are going to take on this challenge is that I want you *to just notice what you notice* about yourself for one full day with few distractions. Notice how you love the freedom from the constant connection. Notice that you feel out of sorts and seem to fumble around. Notice what people actually look like when they speak with you. Notice what you will be able to read between the lines in conversations with family, friends, and co-workers. Most important, notice yourself.

Being engaged in something, whether it's your work, your relationships, or with yourself, means having a current conscious awareness of more than just the obvious that is surrounding you at any given moment. It means giving a damn about what you are doing and being emotionally connected to it. It also means consciously making decisions to give it your all. It's shifting towards re-engagement.

As I started recognizing how dependent we all are on technology, I started doing a little research and read some interesting articles and statistics. Here is a sampling of what I found.

It wasn't all that long ago when families gathered around a radio and listened to a broadcast of *The Shadow,* Groucho Marx, or *The Avenger,* etc. What's not all that long ago? The '30s, '40s, and '50s is not all that long ago when we consider how long humans have been around. Families tuned in every week to listen to the latest in a series of stories about comedy, the Old West, solving crimes, you name it. The original *War of the Worlds* was actually a radio program that went horribly wrong. It was so realistic that people thought the world was actually under attack!

While families were tuning in, they were together. Parents knew where their kids were and what they were doing and with whom. Maybe you'll think or say that times were just simpler and they're more advanced now. This might be true! There are certainly pros and cons to a simpler time before phones, TVs, computers, PDAs, etc.

Ironically, the list is similar, from what I can tell:

The Pros of Life Before Computers, Cell Phones, PDAs, Etc.

• Your world was your neighbourhood/your block, and you knew all your neighbours.
• You rarely moved far from your family.
• It was a *big* deal when something happened.
• It was a *big* deal when your kid went "away" for college.
• It was a *big* deal when someone you knew died.
• Your kids' influences were your family, your friends, and the priest/rabbi/imam.

The Pros of Life Since the Advent of Computers, Cellular, PDAs, Etc.

• Your world is much broader; the Internet allows you to be friends with people all over the world.
• Your ability to move to another city or country for work creates more opportunity for you and your family.
• Most things aren't that big of a deal.
• Kids routinely go away for college.
• We are a little desensitized when it comes to death; we hear and read about it all the time.
• Your kids' influences are on YouTube, Facebook, Twitter, and their own friends.

As for the last point, that's a pro and a con as far as I am concerned. On the one hand, it seems a shame that all these outside factors other than us are influencing our kids. It either means that we are too busy working or it can mean that we are encouraging our kids to explore the world that's out there; after all, we are as well. Of course, this exposes them to dangers that we didn't have growing up and certainly not ones that our parents and grandparents were forced to encounter. It also shows them that there is a world beyond the one they're raised in. We can't always be there to teach them everything.

The downside of this is that kids don't always know when to shut it all off (like us). When they come to the table with their earphones plugged into their ears, we tell them it's disrespectful. But where did they learn it? Yes, folks, they learned that from us, as much as we might hate to admit it.

Turning off your electronic devices during dinner is as much to allow you to detox as it is to show your kids that they are subconsciously using them just like you do.

Transferring this knowledge to your team is simple: Make a point of starting every staff meeting with the proverbial passing of the basket into which team members dump their cell phones. While they'll initially resist, they'll get used to it and comply and actually feel a sense of freedom. How do I know?

Many American and Canadian office workers report that they are distracted at work by their co-workers' usage of their cell phones on the job. We are actually admitting that cell phones are annoying, despite our dependence upon them. Bans were implemented first on Fridays and then, in some companies, full time. Although there was resistance initially, people eventually reported getting more work done.

With that in mind, you can survive one day without yours.

The following is a declaration that you can have your team or family members fill out and sign. It's a list of all the electronic devices we use daily that we will all go without for one day.

Declaration of Technology-Free Fridays

In accordance with our newly implemented Technology-Free Fridays, I agree that in order to a) ensure better productivity, b) admit my dependence upon technology, and c) work toward relinquishing my dependence, I will give up all of my technology devices on Fridays. My goal is to improve relations with my team members and/or family and foster better communication, which I agree is hampered when I am routinely distracted by the buzzing of a cell phone or PDA.

List of Devices That I Am Willing to Relinquish for the Day
(Check All That Apply)

- Cell phone ❏
- BlackBerry (aka CrackBerry) ❏
- iPhone (there's no app for this, just do it!) ❏
- iPod (tuning out with music is not allowed either) ❏
- Pager (yes, some people still carry them) ❏
- iPad (they may be new, but people are using them) ❏
- Laptop ❏
- iPod Touch (you thought you were going to get away with it?) ❏
- Smart phone, Pocket PC, or any other PDA not listed ❏

_____

Print Name

_____

Sign Name

_____

Team Leader/Parent/Witness

Three Quarters of the Way to Love cont.

During this technologically void meeting, John asked every-one to go around the table and recount the last time each team member had experienced an honest meaningful con-versation with someone at work. Tessa could tell most of her colleagues were getting a bit restless, as it had become com-mon practice for them to text and read e-mails while in these weekly staff meetings. Now their boss was asking them to "share."

She felt like she was in a bad '70s movie, and the fright-ening thing was that not one person on her team of eight col-leagues could give an example of a meaningful conversation. The best they could come up with was the card everyone had written for Nancy when she retired last summer

John was acutely aware of the discomfort in the room, so he suggested they go around the table and share an ac-complishment that they are proud about that happened in the past year. But before they could start to "share," he an-nounced, "Oh yeah, and I will be keeping your phones and laptops with me for the next few days. You can use your desk-top computers and the phones that are actually attached to the desks you work on, but that's it.

"Okay, let's start with Jake...."

Chapter Two

COME CLEAN: HOW AUTHENTIC COMMUNICATION CAN BRING OUT THE BEST IN PEOPLE

Now that the only communication device you have left in your arsenal is your natural human ability to communicate, that is what this chapter is all about. How do we improve and increase our authentic communication skills? Keep in mind that being engaged with people at work and home is based on being emotionally attached to the work and the family, and that takes honest skilful communication.

The truth about the truth is, it can sometimes be hurtful. The concept of authenticity has received a significant amount of attention recently as people search for meaning and happiness, particularly in their work lives. How one chooses to live more authentically depends on his or her perspective on authenticity. Like many other popular concepts, people have different views about authenticity, and many people feel strongly about their own views. Some people might assert that an individual is being authentic if they are being completely honest and participating in the here and now. Others might attribute working authentically to the kind of work you do. Does it line up with your strong passions and personal goals? There are others who assert that authenticity involves many other features, including always being present with themselves and others, living completely integrated with your own values and principles, and always feeling complete with meaning or sense of purpose in life. I personally applaud those who can live this way, because it's a very challenging thing to do.

One of my readers sent in this perspective on authentic focus.

Hi Linda,

As I drove home from work in traffic, my phone dead, I had to resort to listening to the radio. I love talk shows. I at least will find something of value and educational. No matter who is talking. The psychologist from the website Radiant Mind was talking. I do not know his name. He was talking about being in the present, being aware. There is no past or future and how enlightening it is to be in the present and focused. They asked him what his purpose was and I was floored to hear how simple it was. He said just living life and enjoying all the beauty and all it has to offer made him happy. How simple. Everyone is running around looking for his or her "purpose." I now have a better understanding of my purpose, and the rest that I do with my life is icing on the cake.

I do not know if this is any "wow" moment for you, but it sure was for me. I have to quit complicating things in my life.

Cheers, Niki

And to add some spice, another reader, Vicki, suggested, "a good lunch-hour encounter with your spouse is a great way to re-energize and focus for the afternoon."

Regardless of others' perspectives on authenticity, it's important for leaders to live and work as authentically as possible—a goal that is usually often difficult to achieve, particularly in large organizations that don't support a more heartfelt approach to work. But if engagement is a real goal and not just lip service, then leaders need to get to the heart of how they communicate. To begin the process, pay attention to what you notice about yourself and communicate with respectful honesty.

From Disconnected to Engaged: Leaders Who Don't Know They Lack Communication Skills

Read the following statements and see what areas of your communication skills need some work. Engagement is based on open honest communication that emotionally connects you to your team and them to you.

1. **I can sense the mood of others by looking at them as we speak.** This reflects on your ability to read people in the moment and helps you decide how to approach the topics.

2. **I let others do most of the talking in conversations.** Doing more than your fair share of the talking is only okay when the other person is very shy and it allows you to ask questions to get them to talk. Great communicators are great listeners.

3. **I am able to resolve problems without losing control of my emotions.** This skill requires being fully aware of your emotions and keeping them in check when the discussion gets heated. When our emotions rise, we lose our ability to think clearly.

4. **I am able to stand in other people's shoes and see their point of view.** Step back and see how people come to their conclusions. This does not mean you have to agree with them. Just see. You will be more respectful in your communication if you do.

5. **When talking to people, I pay attention to their body language (body shifting, facial expressions, hand movement, twitching, etc.).** People often say more with their bodies than with their words.

6. **I know how to find the right words that will clearly express what I want to say.** When your nerves overcome you, it's often difficult to know what to say. Also, if you feel intimidated by the person or group with whom you are communicating, the perfect words will tend to elude you. The more you practice, the better your nerves will be. If you are in a situation where you know you will be nervous, then practice communicating the issues you want to get across. Write them down and refer to your notes.

7. **When I am angry, I can identify that emotion and I can admit it.** This is about being totally self-aware. Being able to notice your emotions and identify how and what you are feeling enables you to metaphorically back away from a situation and see it for what it really is.

8. **I can tell when someone doesn't understand what I'm saying.** When you are skilled at reading body language and know how to ask clarifying questions, you will know if you have been heard and understood.

9. **I am completely at ease when a conversation shifts to the topic of feelings.** Being comfortable with the fact that everyone has feelings and that expressing feelings is the key to being connected to work and home life will put you well on your way to a fully engaged environment.

10. **I express my ideas clearly.** Being able to speak clearly with well thought out ideas and concepts is a skill that takes a lot of practice. This skill is really only mastered by the very few. Most avid readers tend to be clear communicators because they have read the written word so often that it aids in their own expression.

11. **I avoid being caught up in what I have to say and remain aware of the reactions of my listeners.** If you avoid being eager to tell others how great your thoughts are, you won't forget to listen to what other people have to say. Remember, the number one skill of a great communicator is listening.

12. **Even when I know what someone is going to say, I never finish the sentence for him or her.** Finishing the sentences of others can appear as either helping the other person out or just plain bad manners. Many couples who have been together for a while find that they end each other's sentences. Bite your tongue and let the other party finish their thoughts

13. **I rarely misinterpret people's words.** Most misinterpretations come from the tone and body language given

by the other party. Ask clarifying questions if you are getting the wrong information.

14. **I'm comfortable dealing with emotionally charged situations.** Don't worry about this, as emotionally charged situations make most people uncomfortable. Take a breath and just focus on your listening.

15. **I avoid fidgeting while listening to someone talking. I remain focused.** Fidgeting (playing with your hair, watch, or pen) is a signal that you are nervous. Catch yourself and put your hands in your pockets. Focus, like listening, takes practice, so just focus. Choose to take a day when you "overfocus" and see how that goes for you. You will be exhausted, I'm sure.

16. **I am comfortable in most social situations.** I am okay with just talking about "the weather." I don't mind if there is no real point to a conversation. Even analytical and content-driven personalities sometimes simply make small talk.

17. **I find it easy to say what I want in a given moment.** Being engaged with people is all about connecting on the same level of where the other person is. All of us, regardless of our personality styles, need to learn to communicate with all the other styles out there. Practice having casual conversations with people for no other reason than just connecting. You might even meet someone fascinating.

18. I'm comfortable expressing my feelings to others.
Most of us have a difficult time just identifying our feelings, let alone expressing them. We may think we are angry when we are really just hurt and sad, but it just comes out as anger. There are several charts to help you put a label to an emotion. Just do a Google image search for "emotions."

Getting into the Moment

Having the ability to be mindful of how we are communicating is a big part of getting into the moment. It's difficult to listen if your mind is elsewhere. Whether your focus is on the dinner to cook, the action items of yesterday's meeting, the C your kid got in school, it's immaterial. The important thing is to allow yourself to be right where you are at this very moment. Buddhists call it Bodhi, which means "awakening." If you have a history of being unable to stay in the here and now, you are not fully awake. You should be able to turn off whatever is going on and fully engage in what's in front of you.

How does one do this? Some people have to visualize it, others have to "shake it off," and still others might find that they have to talk to themselves. "Okay, Joe is standing in front of me; I need to focus on his needs at this moment." Joe could be a co-worker, your boss, your spouse, or your child. Again, this is immaterial. Chances are, if you have difficulty getting into the moment, you have this difficulty in all areas of your life.

You may have to turn yourself inside out before you understand why you have difficulty in this area. This is not easy, mind you, and it takes practice. Each time you do it, it gets easier. While you're focusing on why you are having difficulty with this, you may want to take steps to stop yourself from focusing on everything that is not in the here and now.

Some people experience some kind of trauma or difficulty before reaching this awakening. What do you say we skip the trauma, the drama, and the agonizing hours of talk therapy and skip ahead to the awakening?

You didn't think this would be easy, did you? Actors have to do it all the time to turn off what was happening as soon as the director yells, "Action!" Having the ability to go from "there" to "here" will take practice. We as spouses, parents, subordinates, bosses, and co-workers wear so many hats that we are actually schooled in multitasking. During interviews, your potential boss will likely ask whether you can do this. Of course, you want to say yes, when in reality the answer is no. The best answer is that we can focus on the here and now and get the job done, and then move on to the next task.

Cutting Down Distractions

Being in the here and now also means cutting down on distractions. Again, this is much easier said than done. This requires us to almost turn off all the things that we are told make us a good team member. We have to be able to wear several hats, be a productive team member, be a leader on this project, a contributor on that one, and still be able to be exemplary in all areas. How can we do this effectively if we are wearing so many hats? The only way to accomplish this is to be able to shut off distractions. This doesn't just mean closing your office door. It also means being able to be in the here and now. The two must go hand in hand. You can't do one without the other. Seems obvious, right? As you're reading this, you are no doubt thinking, "Um, I am not having an epiphany here." No? If that were the case, you can easily turn off your cell phone during meetings and while you're on vacation and focus fully on the here and now.

When you're in a meeting, being focused includes blocking yourself off from your phone. Even if it doesn't ring or vibrate, you know it's there and that at any moment an extremely important call could come in. This means that you're not focused and giving the meeting and the points being made your full attention. This means that you are, if not distracted, open to being distracted. As the saying goes, "Just say no!" Turn it off, look into the eyes of the person who's speaking, listen, and be engaged. That's how you'll be able to be a good contributor and productive team member.

Value-Based Decisions

A challenge for executives and managers comes when thinking about bringing value to a project. Their main objective is often the particular project at hand. Let's look at it this way: if you are reading a book and think of each chapter as individuals, you might get the point, but you won't really until you've reached the end of the book, right? Thinking of things in their totality, their wholeness, rather than in their individual parts can allow you to be a more productive team member and bring more value to your projects.

How often does this happen to you? You're in a meeting with marketers, salespeople, and project managers and each one can only see the project from his or her point of view or that of their department's. To move the project forward requires seeing through all this and how the contributions of each department bring value and are of equal importance. This is much easier said than done. The next time you interact with team members from other departments, allow yourself to see how these departments benefit the whole company. This will surely help you bring better value to your work and the project.

Sometimes bringing value also means not taking every single project that comes across your table. Not all projects are worth championing. Some are better left as concepts. Knowing when to say no brings as much value as seeing a project to its fruition.

Honesty: At What Cost?

How often are you asked your opinion and you've regretted your honesty? Being honest, when asked, is a tough call to make. Some people have no problem offering their opinions regardless of how it makes the recipient feel. Others hesitate and prefer to hold back their feelings. Rather than always jumping in or always beating around the bush, ask yourself what purpose it serves. In other words, each situation has to be weighed separately.

Ask yourself whether your honesty will ultimately benefit or hinder the recipient. If being honest causes more harm than good, ask yourself whether it's really important. If, on the other hand, after weighing things carefully, you decide that the person will only benefit, then go for it.

Dealing with Blind Spots to Avoid Conflicts

If you have ever taken a personality quiz such as DISC (Dominance, Influence, Steadiness, Conscientiousness), Personalysis, Psycho-Geometrics, or the Myers-Briggs Type Indicator, you'll know that these were developed with the understanding of how to approach each personality type. Those who see things in black and white, the social butterfly who loves to hear everyone's opinion and make sure that everyone is counted, and the person who must be direct and be dealt with in a direct manner all require different types of interaction, right? When in the moment, we often forget about this and just forge ahead. Agenda in hand, we approach our co-worker, subordinate, or spouse and fire away! The next thing we know, an eruption ensues and we're standing there wondering why it happened.

This happens more often than not because we forget that it is not about what we say, but rather how the other person hears things. Whether it's someone at work or your spouse or sibling, people often don't hear the way we want them to. These can be blind spots, or simply dealing with people on their terms to avoid conflict. We can avoid so many conflicts if we would stop, take a moment, and ask ourselves how this information is going to be received. If need be, go over it in your mind first, remembering that the person to whom you're speaking communicates differently from you. You can really save hours and days of avoidable drama by doing so.

Revealing and Celebrating All Aspects of Your Team

The pleaser, the leader, the stubborn one, the balanced one, the "whatever" one on your team needs to be heard, recognized, and celebrated. Your team isn't whole unless each member is contributing. Each one brings value to the team. An effective leader understands that the team is dysfunctional if even one member is feeling slighted or ignored. A breakdown occurs and a project cannot move forward until all team members are being heard and celebrated for his or her input. This means trying a different approach rather than dismissing a team member because he is the naysayer and you know he will attempt to set up roadblocks before your milestones. Add it to the agenda. "Bob, I know that at this point you are going to have an objection for why we can't move forward. Let's discuss those reasons and see how we can resolve them right now." Bob will feel better for being recognized rather than the way he usually feels, which is put off and dismissed.

Conversely, knowing that Rudy is a pleaser, always goes along with the majority, specifically address him and say, "Rudy, how do you feel about this point?" Whatever Rudy tells you, ask him to elaborate rather than allow him to just agree. What you will find is that Rudy has quite a well-rehearsed opinion and has been waiting to be asked for it.

As the leader, you will no doubt find yourself in the position of having a second person on the team who feels that she is better suited for that position. Again, rather then dismiss her, which is only going to make her angry and prove her point that she is a better leader, ask her, "Denise, I am having a problem resolving this issue. How would you go about it?" You'll be surprised how you can go from passive-aggressive behaviour to a very productive contributing member who just might teach you something.

Creating a Game Plan for Communication and Conflict

Fostering communication and avoiding conflict are the hallmarks of a good team leader. If a leader brings out and celebrates all the personalities on the team rather than fight them, the team will operate as a whole. Sometimes, taking the team outside of the work environment is required to achieve this.

It's amazing what happens when you leave the office for the day and go bowling or race around in bumper cars or go build something together. These are called team builders for a reason. Watching each member pull together to help build a house for a needy family rather than simply to meet a corporate goal, you can see how each one thinks, operates, and contributes. A good leader observes and contributes to the team simultaneously. Earlier, we discussed how bringing value to the team or project means thinking in terms of the whole impact rather than merely the benefit to oneself. This is one way to put this into action. Your goal is not to complete the project at work and make each team member look good. The goal is ensuring that by day's end a family of five will have a house to call home. All right, this may be a challenge if you've never built a house, but the foundation will have been laid both for the house your team built and for the future of your team.

Three Quarters of the Way to Love cont.

When last we left Jake, he was about to share his greatest accomplishment over the last year. As he quickly scanned his brain, he sensed that Tessa was a little ticked off for his not sending off that three-letter text at the start of the meeting to indicate that getting together after work was a great idea. He knew very well that he was going to have to a) dig himself out of the hole with her and b) make his response interesting enough to capture his "audience." But you see, this presented Jake with a big problem because he isn't the most gregarious of fellows. He detests the notion of sharing anything personal with people at work, and trying to do so to appease his not-quite-new girlfriend, who nobody knew was his girlfriend, was causing a bit of angst in him.

However, he psyched himself up and said the following, all of which completely caught both Tessa and him by surprise. His co-workers were left with their mouths gaping open and wondering just who this man was, because surely aliens scooped Jake up and replaced him with this romantic effusive man. Tessa herself had to hold back the tears, as she had waited for months for Jake to do what he did.

Chapter Three

CREATING A TEAM ENERGY AND ENGAGEMENT PLAN:
LEARN HOW FULL TEAM BUY-IN ENGAGES AND
INSPIRES EVERYONE

According to talent development firm BreakThroughs, Inc., recent research shows that financially stronger companies—defined as those with a return on investment (ROI) of thirty percent or higher—tend to be strong in key measurable competencies of a high-performance team culture. They also say that, on the other hand, financially weaker companies—those with an ROI of nine percent or lower—score low on those same measurements of the competencies necessary to create a high-performance team culture. Basically, strong team culture = strong bottom lines!

What is team culture and how do we create it? Working in teams and avoiding the salvos seems to be the only way that companies can compete and win. Would you agree? No one person has all the answers. If that were the case, the president or CEO of your company wouldn't need you. The marketing team wouldn't need sales, the sales team wouldn't need the engineers, etc. The buzzwords such as *cross-pollination*, *cross-functional*, and the long-standing one, *teamwork*, were created as a means to get buy-in from all teams to move projects forward. Given that decisions affect the entire company, doesn't it make sense to "have a seat at the table"? Creative breakthroughs happen when you've got a team.

The culture of your company's team might be different, depending on the product or service you are selling. If you are a pharmaceutical company, your cross-functional team will have doctors and researchers as well as members of manufacturing, in addition to the usual marketing and sales team members. If you sell nuts and bolts, your engineers and designers are every bit as important as the sales and marketing team members.

The diversity of education, experience, and perspectives of the members of your team create your company and team culture.

This applies to your home team as well. Your daughter is a soccer player and a pianist—she brings a very different perspective than your son who prefers to sit in his room and create science experiments. Both have very different perspectives, and yet each has a valuable opinion and contributes equally.

It's very important for the health of your team and its culture to encourage all to participate, especially those who are naturally reluctant, maybe due to his or her role or personality. A secretary, for instance, may feel her contribution isn't significant, or your son may be introverted.

The bottom line is that high-performance team culture reinforces the organization's mission statement, vision statement, and values by providing a strategic alignment. Alignment leads to improved performance, productivity, and bottom-line results. High-performance team cultures within successful organizations are those that have the following seven interwoven core competencies:

1. Leadership
2. Coaching
3. Teamwork

4. Commitment
5. Clear roles and expectations
6. Communication
7. Trust

You might be asking what creating a strong team culture has to do with energizing a team. Two things, actually. Culture is one of those non-tangible things that seem like the energy of the group. It's the written and unwritten rules, the code of conduct that govern what we do and how we do it. A team without a clear culture can completely drain the life out of its members. However, when culture is fostered, it can be the spirit that keeps you going even when you are exhausted. Here are some of the things you should come to expect from a high-performing team:

• A team that's energized by clear directions;
• When one team member is off mentally, physically, or emotionally, the rest of the team picks up the slack;
• A more holistic and functional team;

Team culture is influenced by the personalities of the members and the leader, the environment in which they work, the nature of the communications they use, the stories they have to tell about the team, their rituals and celebrations, and their shared language.

The final key to a successful highly functioning team is that each member, including the leader, must nurture their self-awareness. This includes how you see yourself in the world and knowing what works and what doesn't in all aspects of your life at work and home. Knowing what you do well and not so well and being able to admit both is crucial when getting to know yourself better.

Your Team/Family Energy Plan

Whether you like it or not, an effective energy plan requires each member of your team to do the following five things:

1. **Move your body.** Get more oxygen flowing through everyone's body more often. This one is *non*-negotiable. Meetings that involve sitting for hours at a time cause sleepiness, boredom, random thoughts that have nothing to do with the meeting, and increased time on mobile devices. Without some physical activity, team members start to "check out" and you've lost creativity and buy-in. It's important to incorporate activities to get the body moving, the blood flowing, and the brain focused. At the very least, get up every hour and move for a few minutes. One of my readers Chrystal of Legal Services added this bit:

    > We have started arranging fun little exercise things to do for the lunch hour—a short run/walk on the sea wall, climbing the stairs in our building, or getting together to meditate to soothing music. That gets us changed from work clothes to exercise gear, and away from the desk, but gives us time to eat—all during the lunch hour. People find the shifting of gears just as beneficial as the exercise value.

2. **Laugh more.** An atmosphere of laughter is mandatory for your home and work life. Imagine the drudgery of

your day when all you can do is work, work, work. The boss is on you every minute to be productive and is reticent to talk about anything personal, regardless of its significance. Your one-on-one meetings with your boss, whether planned or chance meetings, are always work related and can be both boring and filled with negativity.

You no more like it as a subordinate to someone else, so why would you create the same atmosphere for your team? Catch your administrative assistant off guard by telling a joke! When your assistant offers to help you with something, laugh and say, "Lighten up." I guarantee you'll get more productivity out of your staff this way. How do I know? Dr. David Abramis at Cal State University, Long Beach, has studied fun at work for years. He's discovered that people who have fun on the job are more creative, are more productive, are better decision-makers, and get along better with co-workers. They also have fewer absent, late, and sick days than people who aren't having fun. This translates to happier workplaces, where employees are more loyal and productive.

Overall, absenteeism may decrease because people are actually looking forward to going to work. Turnover may decrease as well, as employees feel more content and loyal to the organization. And costs associated with illness may decrease as people experience the positive physiological and psychological benefits of laughter.

3. **Have fun.** There's a direct correlation to fun and bottom-line results. In a recent article on Fortune 100 companies, ninety-three percent of staff at these highly

successful organizations—based on bottom-line results and customer satisfaction surveys—relate the fact that they work in very fun and friendly environments to the company's success.

4. **Maintain a work/life balance on the weekend.** You've been saying for months that you plan to do this, or get to that. The more you fail to get around to it, due to your work responsibilities, the more you build up resentment for your job. And, trust me, it spills over into your home life. Most of us have only two days off a week; use them wisely and productively. And productivity has nothing to do with checking your work PDA. It has nothing to do with monitoring your work e-mail. It has to do with spending time with your family and finishing the jobs you have been promising them that you would finish.

5. **Maintain a work/life balance during the week.** Remember in college how you made sure that you had time to party in between studying and classes? You built it into your week, didn't you? You knew that if you studied all night on Thursday, you could make that party on Saturday, right? When your friends asked you out during the week, you accepted, didn't you? It's important to remember what that did to your psyche. You were more, not less, productive when you took time out of your day to have a little fun. Maybe you caught up with your buddies, called your girlfriend or boyfriend, or went to a movie. While your level of responsibility was nothing like it is now, you can still do this.

Make plans with your spouse, and if you have kids,

show up to their games or other events. Two things will immediately happen if you do these. First, your communication will improve. Second, your kids will be more likely to do what you ask of them because you kept your promise of showing up. If you don't show up, they'll feel slighted, you'll feel guilty, and there's this perpetual anger going around. All for what? Your job? It'll be there tomorrow. Leave work on time, but once in a while, ditch work early!

Being Married to Your Work Is Not a Recipe for Engagement or Trust

It can be tempting to rack up the hours at work, especially if you're trying to earn a promotion or some extra money for a child's education or a dream vacation. For others, working more hours feels necessary to manage the workload.

If you're spending most of your time at work, your home life will likely pay the price. Consider the pros and cons of working extra hours on your work/life balance:

- **Fatigue.** Your ability to think and your eye-hand coordination decrease when you're tired. This means you're less productive and are prone to make more mistakes. These mistakes can lead to injury or costly errors, which would have a negative impact on your professional reputation.

- **Family.** You may miss important events, such as your child's first bike ride, your father's sixtieth birthday, or your high-school reunion. Missing out on important milestones may harm relationships with your loved ones.

- **Trust.** If you are wondering how to build it, keep it, and nurture it, it's rather simple. As a team leader at work or a parent at home, you must lead by example. If you tell your team or family to trust you, to build trust as a team, to maintain more work/life balance, to laugh out loud and stop taking things so seriously, and to take walk breaks and not sit on their butts all day, you have to do something very important: do the same yourself. How can you expect your team or family to trust you if you don't practice what you preach?

Whatever your message is, you have to live it to share it. You have to lead by example. What are the consequences of not doing this? It's simple. Why should your team or family trust anything you say if you can't demonstrate that you believe in it as well?

Here are some tips for building trust:

1. One Friday a month, have a pizza party, go bowling, or do some other fun activity and make it mandatory for staff to leave the office.
2. Celebrate all team members' birthdays that occur each month.
3. In all your staff meetings, acknowledge the accomplishments of one of your team members that was *not* related to their work.
4. If you see your staff working through lunch, discourage it.
5. Encourage staff to go for a walk.
6. Start a walking club—no work talk allowed.
7. Create a non-work talk zone or hour.

8. Create a timer on your e-mail program that reminds you to leave the office.

9. Stop by each of your staff members' offices or cubicles and announce that you're leaving and you *expect* them to do the same.

10. Let them know why you're leaving, e.g., to spend time with your spouse/kids, attend Joey's soccer tournament, have a date, make a bench for your backyard, etc.

Believe it or not, implementing these small changes in your company or department will have a snowball effect. Your team will believe in your word, they'll be more productive, and they'll be more inclined to share some of their ideas and be better and more productive team members.

Create a Culture of Trust

Executive leaders communicate the clear expectation that they expect teamwork and collaboration. They follow up and do what they say they are going to do. Also, they don't watch clocks and tend to produce more results than the rest of the company and do not have the expectation that everyone should work as hard as they do. They do expect every team member to work to his or her absolute best abilities.

Every leader should revisit what it is like to do frontline work again. They assist and help with even the smallest of tasks. The recent TV hit *Undercover Boss* has shown this to be highly successful. This show has proven how important it is for all executives to go back to the front lines and see how the teams and operations really work. You will be surprised how tired you will be after a day of doing frontline work again, and you will appreciate your staff more.

The organization members talk about and identify the value of a teamwork culture. They are either talking about and identifying with the value or they are trashing it.

Teamwork is rewarded and recognized. Each leader must find out how each member wants to be recognized and then reward them in that way. A one-size-fits-all staff reward system is usually ineffective.

Important stories that people discuss within the company emphasize teamwork. This is ever so clear if you chat with a union member who has ever walked with union brothers or sisters on a strike line. They will remember and tell those stories forever, so think about creating stories within your team that will be told ten or twenty years from now. Now that's building *team trust culture.*

You will not build teamwork by *just* "retreating" as a group for a couple of days each year, although there are many benefits of taking a few days away from the office with your team and your family (remember all your getaways). Think of team building as something you do every single day. Quite simply, trust takes time. In other words, if you aren't walking the walk every day of the week, that offsite team building to create and foster your team is a complete waste of time. Your team members will learn that you aren't a person of your word.

Three Quarters of the Way to Love cont.

Jaws were still gaping and some continued dragging on the floor. Nobody could possibly have followed up and shared an accomplishment such as the one Jake expressed like a series of cannonballs. Are you wondering what happened? Indeed, your mind is racing and you've already jumped to conclusions, haven't you?

Chapter Four

DUNG IT OUT! HOW THE ENVIRONMENT YOU
WORK/LIVE IN AFFECTS
YOUR ENGAGEMENT, ENERGY, AND BOTTOM-LINE
OUTCOMES

Take an honest open-eyed look at where you work and live. According to declutter expert Peter Walsh, getting organized comes from a place of respect. If you respect yourself, you will respect the place where you work, the place where you create, and, most important, the place where you lay your head at night. Walsh also indicates that the best way to start this "cleaning out" is to ask yourself, "What is the vision of your best life?"

Get your "Dung It Out Journal" and take some notes:

- When you were a teenager dreaming of your life as an adult, what did you envision for yourself?
- What kind of work did you see yourself doing?
- What did the place you would call home look like? What types of furnishings were you surrounded by?
- Would you be working in an office, getting dressed up each day in business clothes, or working in a career that uses your hands and perhaps gets you a bit dirty each day?

I am asking you to go back and remember here, so you have a bit of groundwork to build on. As you have worked into your career and home life, have any of these things worked out as you had dreamed they would? Is the life you are living better than or not as good as the one you dreamed of? Sometimes these things are not quantitative, but do your best.

As you read this, you might be in your current office or living room. If you are, I want you to take a good look around, and I mean really look.

- Do you enjoy being in this space? Are you productive and comfortable in this space?
- Do you connect well with people in this space?
- Does the furniture need dusting? How are the floors?

And I don't want the thoughts of how your company hires a cleaning crew, or how you pay someone at home to do this and so you needn't be concerned with this. *Wrong* answer! I also get someone to come into my home to clean every two or three weeks, but my family and I still need to maintain the place throughout those days when she's not there.

I keep referring to both your home and work life, but you will have to choose which area of your life right now with which you need to be more engaged. If it's both, choose one to work on for the time being.

What is the vision you have of yourself right now that is the *best* of *you?* For the sake of focus, please choose either at home or at work. How might you start to respect yourself more and clean up your space so the best *you* can emerge? I have always joked about how I don't see the mess or how dirty my fridge is until I have company over. I get used to the mess and then I just don't see it.

As we all know, there are always two sides to every story. Let's look at the benefits, downsides, and payoffs for being overly clean and overly messy.

A Case for Some Dirty Work

My dad always had a saying when we were growing up that "pigs don't get fat in clean water." Now I am not sure if that is a strong argument to keep the dirt under your nails, but according to the website Cleaning Expert, although we all know that cleanliness is next to godliness, it's very possible to go overboard and take things to extremes. "Over-cleaning" can actually do more harm than good and even cause specific dangers to you and your family. Keeping a good balance between good hygiene and obsessive-compulsive cleaning is important.

Here are just a few reasons to find a balance for both arguments. Keep in mind that we are trying to create work and home environments that will be inspiring, productive, and fun places in which to work and create.

Allergies and Autoimmune Reactions

In industrialized countries, high hygiene standards and constant cleaning with harsh chemical products have created an overly antiseptic environment, resulting in a surge of allergies and autoimmune diseases. For example, research has found that in some inner cities allergies in children have gone from being a rare occurrence to being something that affects nearly half of children living there.

Protecting children from exposure to the everyday bacteria, viruses, and fungi they would normally encounter means that their immune systems never learned to mature and deal with these threats. They become oversensitive to many substances in the environment. By keeping things too clean, you're actually increasing your children's risks of contracting conditions such as asthma and eczema. Case in point: have you been to a developing country lately? Even after I took the anti-cholera and anti-diarrhea immunizations, I still got wickedly sick when I visited Nepal last November. The doctor actually laughed at me when I told him I had received the immunizations. I think his words were, "Our bugs laugh at your Western medications. That will be one hundred USD, thank you!" And, of course, at that point I would have paid anything to feel better.

Allowing both us and our children to indulge in some "messy dirty activities," such as finger painting or playing at a park, can provide important learning experiences while building up our immune systems.

While looking at the pros and cons of cleaning—and what I really mean is dunging out—let's address cleaning here for just another moment. I came across a number of sites warning us all on the dangerous effects of using toxic cleaning products. Author Lorie Dwornick covers how dangerous our basic home cleaning products really are. It's a miracle that any of us have any energy, let alone have the benefit of being engaged in our daily lives. Here's what she has to say:

> Cleaning products often contain harmful chemicals that are not listed on the label. Only one percent of toxins are required to be listed on labels. This is mainly because the products don't make any claims about safety. Companies can also classify them as "trade secrets" to avoid listing them. Many of the ingredients labelled "inert" are actually more toxic than the active ingredients.

When considering cleaning products, they should be:

- Biodegradable
- Formulated without dye
- Non-flammable
- Contain no ammonia, acids, alkalis, solvents, phosphates, chlorine, nitrates, borates, or volatile organic compounds

So with this advice in mind, we all need to make choices that will benefit our homes, families, and the planet. Okay, now go and conquer the world!

Messy not Dirty

The two most popular New Year's resolutions are to lose weight and to get organized. If you are starting to look around and realize that you are failing on the getting organized part, you are in good company there too. Most resolutions fail within six weeks. We all revert to the familiar and comfortable, whether that includes junk food or creating and living in a mess.

I read a review of the book *A Perfect Mess: The Hidden Benefits of Disorder* by Eric Abrahamson and David H. Freedman that said the premise seems to be that messes are okay, perfectionism is the enemy, and neatness is overrated. I looked around my house and saw the cluttered bookcase; mail piled up in at least three locations; and the overlapping layers of notes, business cards, and photos along with a motley crew of magnets littering the fridge and heaved a sigh of relief. Maybe getting organized was a waste of time. And note to self: *just close the door to the laundry room; I'll fold that sometime, later...maybe.*

According to Abrahamson and Freedman, creativity often resides in clutter. They call it "finding serendipitous connections between disparate documents." One example in praise of messiness is the discovery of penicillin from mouldy neglected petri dishes. Too bad I can't find something miraculous from the mould on old jars of jam in my fridge. I would argue that creativity has a tough time surfacing in a mess and that a clean canvas is what's needed to produce greatness. But this is why we are examining both sides of this argument in this section on dunging it out.

Associated Content contributor Marsha Raasch recently decided to do some research into the worlds of "neat freaks" vs. "messies." Here are some things she discovered:

- **Perfectionism is the enemy.** A blind reliance on a certain filing or organization system can often mask an internal chaos and insecurity. I have always stated that there are two types of perfectionists. And perfectionism is a disease we just have to get over. It is all based on insecurity, if we weren't insecure about something, we would just leave it alone. The first type of perfectionist is a person who has high standards for themselves and the second type is a person who has high standards for themselves and everyone else around them. The second type tends to live a lonely life as they find everyone around them backs away because they can't measure up and, quite frankly, everything in life is messy.

- **Being too neat wastes time.** According to Raasch, for some of us organizers, time is as precious a commodity as clean space. Spending time obsessively colour coding a filing system, moving things from one pile to another, or sorting underwear into piles of weekday versus weekend wear just doesn't make sense. According to me (who's not a very organized person), just get it in the right drawer. Now that's organized!

- **Messy is not the same as disorganized.** If you have little trouble locating documents on your desk, what difference does it make if the corners line up at sharp angles? People with a messy work environment are often more efficient because they don't spend time filing and then finding the same piece of paper several times a day.

We are more creative and can relax our minds to find innovative answers when piles and bits of paper do not distract us in our sight lines. The bottom line is, if the system you currently use is working for you, then fly at it. If not, choose what you need to do to be the most effective, relaxed, and creative person you want to be. And don't beat yourself up trying to be neater or more easygoing.

A Case for Rolling Up Your Sleeves to Clean: This Is for Your Work or Home Team

You need an honest assessment to get you started. I want you to open up every closet at home and at work. Ask yourself: do you like what you see? If all your closets were left open and storage room doors taken off, and a bunch of friends came over to your house, or some of your most cherished or potential clients came over for a meeting at your workplace, would you be embarrassed?

Where to Start

At home, tackle your junk drawer. I need you to pick an hour to do this task. You will need a garbage bag and access to your recycling box. Pull out the junk drawer and just look at what's in it—all the gadgets, pens, pencils, twist ties, coupons, etc. For every item, do the six-month test. Have you used this item in the past six months? If not, chuck it, recycle it, or give it away.

When you have difficulty throwing something out, even though you have not used it for over six months, there are deeper issues holding you back. A few of the issues you can consider are perfectionism, fear, emotional attachment, and guilt.

If you are a perfectionist and you know it, you will have difficulty throwing things away because you will fear that you won't make the right decision on each item, so you won't make any decision at all. Fear of making mistakes can be paralyzing because we think we will regret throwing something out and we might look for it later. In reality, we most likely won't. Honestly, when was the last time you used your VCR? And what if Aunt Sally comes over and you can't bring out the serving plate she gave you for your wedding twenty years ago? You know, the one you never used and forgot was actually in your pantry. Who wants that guilt? Below are some tips to help you chuck things out:

- **Ask yourself: Will you really use this item? Honestly? When?** Just keep getting more honest with yourself.
- **More isn't necessarily better.** Throw out the two dozen twist ties already!
- **Categorize items into piles.** Keep it, donate it, sell it, or

chuck it.

- **Don't overthink.** Use my "don't think" method of getting things done. In my last book, *Shift or Get Off the Pot*, I wrote a whole section on not thinking too much. Use it for the dung out. Do not overthink things. When your brain kicks into overdrive, just keep repeating to yourself, "Don't think, don't think, don't think…" as you throw out the items. Trust me, it works.
- **Learn to get past some of the imperfections—it's not just okay to make mistakes; it's mandatory.**
- **Follow the OHIO rule: Only Handle It Once.**
- **Momentum is an awesome force.** Keep the cleaning ball rolling and just keep chucking things out. You will feel awesome when it's done.
- **If you need help, ask for it.** For example, I am really good at chucking things, so I like helping people get rid of stuff. Which of your friends can help you make some decisions?

Once you have completed this task, thoroughly clean out the drawer, washing any inserted organizer trays, and put back any items that passed the six-month test. Voila! Now make a few notes in your journal about how you felt while cleaning out that one drawer.

At work, I would like you to do the same thing if you have one of these drawers or closets or rooms in your office.

Frankly, you need open organized space to be creative and engaged—end of story! It is time to "spring clean" even if it's November. This means you must open and leave open every closet at work (and/or home) until you dung it out. You also need to clean out the files on your computer. Perhaps at one of your next meetings you can have a quick discussion as to why we hold onto stuff that no longer has value. What else at work are you holding onto that no longer has value? Some examples may include old files, promo material, old campaigns, old material on your company website, or policies that were written back in the '80s.

If you are not quite convinced of why you should declutter, here are just a few more reasons. Journalist Patricia Cook from Associated Content cites five good reasons why we could all use a good dunging out:

1. It looks better when you are done.
2. You save time, not having to find things in the clutter.
3. You become more productive (see number two).
4. Being organized saves you money, and sometimes makes you money. Have you ever found coupons and gift certificates in a pile of papers?
5. The most important reason to dung out: it gives you an emotional lift.

Start four piles:

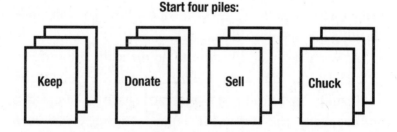

Block off a certain amount of time for this task. All team members are to do this task at the same time, so plan a "get dirty" day. Bring whatever you need: boxes, packing tape, garbage and recycling bags, brooms, dusting rags, etc. You will all feel lighter when you're done. If you're resistant because you have cleaners who come in and do this for you, then give them the week off.

So go to town. Bring some good coffee and crank up the music. When you're done, everyone should go out for beer and wings. Well, that's what I would choose to do. This is also a very good team-building activity.

Three Quarters of the Way to Love cont.

Jake and Tessa have been working through this relationship thing for months. It started on a subway ride, and for some time now they'd been seeing each other. At some point, though they never verbally expressed it, it became an exclusive thing. Tessa knew that if she were to declare her feelings for Jake, he'd run in the other direction. Jake, you see, is a man who is typical of many who have difficulty with both identifying and expressing his feelings. It would be an understatement to suggest that he was not in touch with them.

Tessa knew early on that she felt something more than lust. The problem was that they'd gone too far too quickly and this caused Jake to put the breaks on, so much so that Tessa had been feeling as if he wanted to break things off. Tessa, a woman not shy to express her feelings, was having a very difficult time with this one. She knew he was special, but she also knew that if she pushed too much, she'd lose him.

Instead, she just allowed him to take the lead. This proved difficult over time, as it was at a standstill. One would go to the other's apartment and they'd spend the night together, but it soon seemed strange to her. She had even overlooked how messy Jake kept his place, but even that was starting to bother her. She wanted to tell him to clean up but didn't want to hurt his feelings. Tessa loved the way Jake was able to express himself non-verbally, but at some point, she had to ask, "Is this all there is?"

Don't be fooled! Jake is hot! Women often turned heads when they'd see him in the street. Jake was seemingly oblivious to all this attention, which, of course, made him even more attractive to Tessa.

Tessa's text today at the start of the meeting was her finally working up the nerve to clarify where things were going, and if they weren't moving forward, she was considering ending things. When Jake didn't respond, she got angry. However, as you know, something happened to turn things around for her. She's fighting off tears, and jaws are dragging and tongues will be soon be wagging. And Jake, shy and introverted as he is, didn't care! He felt more alive than he had in years!

For months now, Jake was wondering more and more why Tessa had agreed to start things so quickly. As he got to know her, he realized that the way they jumped into things was seemingly contradictory to her personality. Headstrong, practical, and indeed driven to achieve a lot in her life, this didn't "jive" with the woman who nearly attacked him on their first date.

She was not afraid of anything! She tried anything, and yet Jake was, as he learned, the one less inclined to try new things. But where was this leading them?

Chapter Five

THE POWER OF GETTING TO KNOW EACH OTHER

The most important thing that needs to happen for teams to truly bond is to get to know each other. We are acutely aware that the most important thing a team leader can do to engage and get the most out of the team is to foster a place of trust and openness. I am not just speaking about our daily "chores" at work, but also who we all really are. We are not the sum of our job descriptions. Ask your co-workers about their other interests and you will discover one is a writer, another is an artist, a third should have been a landscape designer, and still a fourth is a quiltmaker.

Ask your team to bring in pictures of themselves doing their hobbies, engaged in their personal interests, etc. It's important that your instructions indicate that you are creating a "Team Board" and that they should bring in copies that they don't mind parting with and displaying.

In your next staff meeting, which will be devoted entirely to this activity, the first agenda item should be "What does *team* mean to you?" Get your journal and be prepared, as the team leader, to start writing.

Have your team create a mural or poster of their answers to the question along with clipped out favourite quotations, funky words, and other pictures from magazines. Include the personal photos they have all brought in. When this is complete, have each member of your team talk about what part of the poster they like the most and why. Then just sit back and watch how it unfolds.

As the leader, you *must* be part of the creation of this poster, and take notes of what is important to the various members on your team. As you're sharing what's important to you about the creation of the board, ask another team member, not your assistant, to take notes. Your assistant should not be your assistant for one meeting for a change. It is imperative that you are all equals, regardless of title.

Over the coming months and even years that you are fortunate to have your team intact, these insights will be invaluable to you. You'll use them to motivate, to help foster the best team, and to create a successful team and successful individual team members. Consider appointing "engagement specialists" for the next year. Have them create a plan of ideas and activities to keep the team efforts and energy moving forward. The more you take part in these activities as a team, the more success you will have on your team. Again regardless of title, encourage anyone to volunteer for this committee. It's important to get a mix of people.

Over time, compare your team to other teams in your company that don't encourage this type of activity and don't see each team member as being equal, regardless of title, and see how functional or dysfunctional each team is. I guarantee that you'll see a difference between yours and theirs.

I have done this activity with every kind of team and it is a wonderful way to re-inspire, re-energize, and re-engage the people you work beside every day.

Personality Differences: Working with and Getting the Most Out of a Variety of Styles

It's important to be comfortable standing in your own skin.

What shape are you in? No, this didn't suddenly morph into a diet book. I mean the question quite literally. What *shape* are you in? My guess is that, like me, you are thirtysomething. Maybe you are twentysomething, fortysomething, fiftysomething, and maybe even sixtysomething. But here's what I came to realize at around thirty-eight: This thing (body) I've been given…is what I have to work with. That's it! Epiphany? Maybe. Am I unique? Hardly! We all come to this conclusion at some point.

It's a rite of passage, we all have to experience, I suppose—this giving up of the charade and being honest about who and where we really are. Although it varies by person, most of us between thirty-five and forty-five wake up and look in the mirror and ask ourselves, "Is this what I've got to work with?" The majority of us come to terms with it.

Now is the time to spend our energy on the other things besides trying to mould ourselves into something that we just aren't. Part of striving to be more connected with the people we work and live with is allowing ourselves to understand the basics of human behaviour. What I always find funny no matter where I go or whom I meet is that people are all very different, but we are also quite predictable, which, for me, is where the humour creeps in.

Maybe you've heard the expression "Love the skin you're in." Well, it applies here. We need to be comfortable living in our own skin. It's not as if there's some kind of do-over button or a trade up to a newer model. Maybe you are tall, short, thin, chubby, blonde, grey, brunette, or bald—well, this is it. I say get over it. Accept it all and be happy. The sooner we all do this, the happier we will be. So many of us exert enormous amounts of energy trying to be something we're not. If you are truly going after the ultimate goal of happiness, you must get over yourself.

With that in mind, let's take a look at how similar—and how different—we really are by examining the four basic types of human personalities:

1. Circle
2. Squiggle
3. Triangle
4. Box

This personality measure is called Psycho-Geometrics. It's been used by companies for years. It has no scientific basis but is so spot on that it's frighteningly funny. Before we begin, here is a quick chart showing what I have found out about people over the past twenty years. Although we are all different, we are very predictable. To me, this is what makes humans so humorous.

The Relater

- Relationship oriented but slower, more direct
- Very good at building trust — takes them time — once a friend, a friend forever
- Good listener
- Good people skills
- Fear of not being included
- HR people
- Steady
- Want to stay with people for a while
- Don't like conflict
- We go to them to cry on their shoulders
- Lots of pictures, candles, dried flowers
- Stressed by pushy behaviour

The Socializer

- Open to too open in relationships
- Love spotlight, high energy, dynamic
- Inactive
- Persuasive
- Great energy at beginning of projects
- Easily bored
- Not good at working alone
- Lack follow through
- Need to be made accountable
- Impatient
- Love the big picture
- Don't buy cars — they wear them
- Motto — "Here for a good time, not a long time"

The Thinker

- Person who is self-contained and on purpose with their tasks
- High attention to detail, analytical
- Like processes, ask "how does that work"
- Very accurate, cautious
- Great follow through — they finish projects that socializers start
- Like to work independently
- Paralysis by analysis
- Procrastinate for fear of making mistakes
- Take lots of pride in their work
- Double checkers — measure twice, cut once (or measure 6 times, cut maybe)
- Stress over surprises, mistakes, and last minute changes
- Need to work on their "change readiness" skills

The Director

- Fast paced and task oriented
- In control and in charge
- Get things done by telling, not asking
- Step on toes, but don't realize it
- Motivated by results and bottom line
- Dominant
- Poor listeners
- Stressed by people who waste time
- Motto — "When I want your opinion, I'll give it to you"

Choose a symbol that reflects your own personality more than any of the others. You may have elements from a couple of them; you may even have elements from three of them. I've never met anyone who likes all four. If you are staring at them all and saying, "Hum, I don't like any of them!" Well, let me just tell you that you are a triangle.

If you resemble the circle, you're a relater/supporter. I always say I should start with these folks, as being excluded is their biggest fear. They are the best communicators because they actually listen—they really do care about the rest of us. They wear their hearts on their sleeves and can tell with a quick glance at their calendars whose birthday, anniversary, or retirement is coming up, as they have all this info documented in their Day-timers. There is just something about their look that says, "Hug me." Their offices usually have dried flowers, candy dishes, and pictures of all their kids, their kids' kids, and, of course, every pet they've ever had. They have a tough time with the word *no*. Whenever they say it, they feel guilty. As a group, they make up about twenty percent of the population.

If you resemble the squiggle, you're a socializer/promoter. These folks are here for a good time, not a long time. Everything to them is a window of opportunity. Fun, fun, fun, that's their lifelong motto. They don't take no for an answer. Actually, they normally don't ask permission in the first place; they just do whatever they want and beg for forgiveness afterward. They also find themselves thinking, "I've gotten by on personality this long. Let's just see if I can push this one more day." Their biggest fear is boredom.

That and, of course, not being invited to the party. They have great energy and enthusiasm for almost everything but lack the discipline to follow up and focus. They make their decisions based on emotion and they make them fast. This group makes up the majority of the population—about seventy-five percent.

If you resemble the triangle, you're a thinker/analyzer. People who like to figure things out are attracted to this shape because it's the most mathematical. They are great researchers: they are very resourceful and love gathering information. I always like to say that information gathering to them is an erotic experience, as they tend to gather, and gather, and gather info. They clip coupons and, more than likely, have a coupon wallet organizer. They comparison shop and even figure out how much gas they will use if they drive to one store or another to make a purchase they have pondered for a few months. They tend not to believe anything until they see some stats, preferably accompanied by a graph. Their biggest fear is making a mistake, so they will do and redo and redo. They base their decisions on information, but they like making decisions slowly, just to make sure they don't make mistakes. In most crowds, they make up about three to five percent of the population.

If you resemble the box, you're a director/controller. These folks like structure. They like everything in its place, and everything has a place. They like making their decisions based on information and they make them fast. They do not like talking about personal stuff at work and really don't feel it belongs there. Their biggest fear is being out of control, or at least appearing to be out of control. They are great visionaries and can lead and push their teams to do their best. They are structured and well organized. In most crowds, they make up less than one percent of the population, but they wish everyone were more like them.

Do you see yourself in these descriptions? If you knew immediately who you were, that's fabulous! If you haven't done so already, it will take far less time to drop the charade and get on with living in your shape. If you are still waffling between shapes, I am not sure what to tell you.

Here's what I do know: You have always known who you are and what your basic style is. For some reason, it takes some of us longer than others to accept that we don't change, and we therefore delay going after that ultimate goal of "happiness." I still say get over yourself and start being just you more often.

Save your energy for the cold days. Don't get me wrong, all of us wear different facades at different times in our lives. Get comfortable in your own skin; it takes too much energy to keep wearing a mask. Deepak Chopra says, "Our greatest purpose is to be ourselves." As I like to say, "The rest is just details."

It's a rite of passage we all have to experience, I suppose, this giving up of the charade and being honest about who and where we really are. This one action will bring you towards a more engaged workplace and home life.

Engaged Communication Skills

Working with the Relater/Supporter (Circle)

Buying style: Requires time and uses feelings

Psychological need: Association

Expectation from you: Sincerity

Dislikes: Being left out

Tips for working with the relater/supporter:

- Break the ice with a personal comment.
- Show a sincere interest in relaters as people; search for common ground.
- Emphasize the benefit to the relater's company, family, or organization.
- Do not come on too strong, too quickly, or in a manner that would be perceived as pressuring a relater.
- Do not debate or argue with the relater.
- Spend plenty of time qualifying the relater by asking many questions.
- Demonstrate that you have their best interests at heart.

Working with the Socializer/Promoter (Squiggle)

Buying style: Buys quickly and uses feelings

Psychological need: Status

Expectation from you: Enthusiasm

Dislikes: Embarrassment

Tips for working with a socializer/promoter:

- Keep your energy level high and the pace of your presentation moving quickly.
- Carefully keep the presentation on track. The socializer will tend to get off topic, and must be subtly lead back.

- Emphasize the product or service in terms of result and status.
- Terms such as "state of the art" or "fastest available" will appeal to a socializer.

Working with the Thinker/Analyzer (Triangle)

Buying style: Requires time and uses information
Psychological need: Security
Expectation from you: Product knowledge
Dislikes: Hype
Tips for working with a thinker/analyzer:

- Provide a complete and logically laid out presentation.
- Do not rush thinkers, allow them to take the time they need.
- Back up your claims with evidence, facts, and figures— avoid gimmicks!

Working with the Director/Controller (Box)

Buying style: Buys quickly and uses information
Psychological need: Control
Expectation from you: Stick to business
Dislikes: Being manipulated
Tips for working with a director/controller:

- Give a clear concise overview of the presentation before going into detail.
- Provide alternative choices to allow the director to retain a feeling of control.
- Focus your information on the end use, the overall result, and the reaching of goals with the help of your product or service.

- Do not provide unnecessary details.

Basic Team Engagement Strategies

As you can see, we all prefer to communicate in ways that suit our personalities. But to truly be effective as a team, we need to take an open look at all team members and consider creative ways to communicate. Consider these tips to ensure each team member's efforts are effective and successful:

- Clearly communicate the team's performance and outcomes.
- Ensure team members understand why they are participating and that they know how their responsibilities fit in with the team and company goals.
- Give each member enough freedom and empowerment to accomplish the team's objectives.
- Provide rewards and recognition when teams are successful. To really boost their effectiveness and get them engaged, ask each member how they want to be recognized. They will all give you a different answer, and you, the leader, need to know this.

Personal Roles and Values: How They Affect Decision Making, Productivity, and Engagement

Think about the complexity of what you've got going on right now. Work teams have a complex mix of people, and each of these people fulfills a diverse set of roles both at work and at home. This needn't be an overwhelming predicament, but rather an exciting opportunity to really get to know a mosaic of people and the roles they play. For example, many of us play these roles:

- Parent
- Spouse
- Sister
- Brother
- Daughter
- Son
- Sandwich maker
- Storyteller
- Homework taskmaster
- Taxi driver
- First-aid attendant
- Cook
- Grocery shopper
- Friend
- Boss
- Frontline worker
- Coach
- Brownie or Cub Scout leader
- Church member
- Etc.
- Oh, and don't forget the staff party organizer

Unfortunately, most of us pile so much "stuff" on our plates that we have difficulty breathing let alone being engaged! Although most of us find it easy to blame the world for our overabundance of duties, the truth is, we should be pointing the finger at ourselves. We honestly believe that by taking it all on, we are somehow contributing to the betterment of whatever we are saying yes to. In reality, I believe we pile so much on our plates, that the pile itself becomes an excuse.

We have so much happening that we can't seem to find the energy to pull ourselves out of bed each morning.

We routinely set ourselves up for failure because we're much more comfortable bailing out on this duty or that project or this party or that commitment because, well, look at all this "stuff" we have to accomplish! How could anyone honestly do all the things we've taken on? In the meantime, even as we struggle with our sanity, let alone our success, we look great to the outside world and come off as such a giving person, one who's there for everyone. It is time to simply stop the madness.

Let me suggest that it's time to prioritize things in your life. Ask yourself: "What roles am I fulfilling that truly bring me joy and energy?" You should be concentrating on that "stuff." Maybe you really enjoy playing chauffeur with the kids, taking them back and forth to soccer practice, piano lessons, and Girl Scouts. Maybe you like the time you're spending together and you're really "on" and "most alive" when you're with the kids. Then, by all means, have at it!

However, if the thought of planning the office party every year sets you in a panic, why on earth would you volunteer to plan it? Do you fear job security if you don't do it? My colleague Patricia Morgan gave a great gift one day when she put it this way: "The next time you don't want to take something on, simply reply with, 'Today is not a good day for me to say yes!'" Maybe there's someone not as inclined to verbalize his or her excitement over the task who's waiting in the wings just dying to take over for you. Why not give him or her a chance?

Embrace the duties that truly bring you joy and add to your life. Seriously consider letting go of the others. Now, I know if parenting is draining you right now, this is one we can't necessarily let go of, but could you do it slightly differently?

Try using the "C" word once in awhile and *compromise*—you, your children, your spouse, your co-workers, your neighbours will all be better off when you do less stuff and do it better!

A Stripped Down You: Ranking the Roles You Play

Maybe you've heard the expression, "Life is a buffet, a free-for-all that we are encouraged to sample and taste to our heart's content." But what usually happens at a buffet? We stand there like a deer in the headlights, overwhelmed by all the possibilities. Then we shift from "deer in the headlights" mode to "kid in a candy store," grabbing everything and anything in sight, just to make sure we get it all in. And after we've sampled everything at least once, we then move into what I call the "antacid phase," looking near and far for the nearest bottle of Tums!

This is what tends to happen in our lives; we say yes to everyone to the point where we often find ourselves saying no to ourselves. Unfortunately, there is no antacid strong enough to douse all that stress and resentment we feel as a result. And on top of the resentment is a feeling that we no longer recognize who is saying yes to everyone!

One of my favourite movies of all time is *Shirley Valentine,* whose main character Shirley Bradshaw starts to question who she has become and, more important, where she has gone. She sets off on a quest, in her mid-life, to find herself again. She desperately wants to be re-engaged and energized for the life she longs for, but for her to do this, she needs to be honest with herself. The same applies to you, and it takes some courage with a big spoonful of humility.

It's time to take a few of those "junk food" items off your current plate of responsibilities. The following exercise will help you prioritize the roles you play and how they affect you. The following are several roles we take on in our lives, for better or for worse. Now go through each one and rate whether the role is an energizing or draining role in your life right now:

Role	Energizing	Draining
Parent		
Sibling		
Daughter/son		
Nurse help		
Friend		
Volunteer		
Service club member		
Church member		
Athlete		
Boss		
Artist		
Crafty person		
Driver		
Neighbourhood cook		
Business partner		
Part-time employee		
Student		
Babysitter		
Other		

Choose three roles on your list that no longer give you joy and plan a guilt-free exit strategy. Trust me, you'll love yourself for it.

Being Engaged and Energized Requires Knowing Who and What You Are

In this section of the book, you have been taking an honest snapshot of your life. Don't just take "your best side" and smile at the pretty picture in the frame; use the wide lens and take a snapshot of yourself, warts and all. Record all that is good, all that could use some improvement, and perhaps even a few things that need a lot of work.

It's amazing how long we can go just seeing ourselves as we want ourselves to be: the capable, helpful, together, hip, cool, friendly, gracious, selfless soul who's always up for just one more favour, task, role, or duty. Meanwhile, we're frazzled to the breaking point, lacking sleep and showing it on every inch of our puffy sleep-deprived faces.

I realize that it's difficult to trust the photographer when you're the one taking the picture, so don't bother. Ask friends and family for an honest assessment of you as well. Then ask yourself the following nine questions to help discover the true you hiding underneath that big heaping pile of duties:

1. How would your friends describe you in each of these roles?
2. How do your work colleagues describe you?
3. How would you describe yourself?
4. What roles energize you?
5. What roles would you like to drop if you could?

6. Can you redefine yourself in any of these roles?
7. Are you truly yourself when you play these roles and are you more *you* in some than in others?
8. Why is that?
9. What are some common values that shine when you are more yourself in any of these roles?

You really can't go forward from here unless you know who's taking the journey. In other words, you can only be successful when you know *who* and *what* you are.

Understand and Apply Your Values

With so many people depending on us, it's difficult to find the time to get to know ourselves, isn't it? But find the time we must. Since I know time is limited, it's important to also use that time wisely. That is why I've created this quick list of values to help you find out exactly where you stand and what you stand for.

Why values? You must know the values you stand for, if success and happiness are important to you. Most of us are not clear about our values and find we flounder when opportunities come our way. We ask ourselves, "Should I do it or not?" Meanwhile, temptation creeps in when the option is of little value and opportunity slips by. There's a saying that goes "If you know what you want, you can say *no* to what you don't want."

How can we tell the difference if we don't know the difference? When we are clear about how we see ourselves and the values we respect, making decisions becomes easier, quicker, and is more beneficial for all involved. Make a list of all the things you value in your home and work life so that decision-making becomes easier and more satisfying. Below are a few examples of values you might find important:

- Achievement
- Friendship
- Physical challenges
- Advancement and promotion
- Growth
- Adventure
- Having a family
- Power and authority
- Affection (love and caring)
- Charity
- Privacy
- Art
- Helping society
- Public service
- Challenging problems
- Honesty
- Change and variety
- Independence
- Quality
- Close relationships
- Influencing others
- Quality relationships
- Community
- Inner harmony
- Recognition (respect from others, status)
- Competence
- Integrity

- Religion
- Competition
- Cooperation
- Involvement
- Responsibility and accountability
- Country
- Job tranquility
- Security
- Creativity
- Knowledge
- Self-respect
- Decisiveness
- Leadership
- Serenity
- Democracy
- Location
- Sophistication
- Ecological awareness
- Loyalty
- Stability
- Economic security
- Market position
- Status/reputation
- Effectiveness
- Meaningful work
- Supervising others
- Efficiency
- Merit
- Time freedom
- Ethical practice
- Money

- Truth
- Excellence
- Nature
- Wealth

What's next? First, look at the list. If you feel there are others you want to add to it, by all means do so. Next, choose twenty values from this list. Whittle it down to your top ten, then your top five. Now when making daily decisions for your home and work life, reflect on your list. The truth is that when your life feels out of balance, it means you have prioritized things that do not fall in line with the values you have set for yourself.

This list ticking may take time at first, and practice. But don't all good habits?

Now, in just three minutes, write down the answers to this question: What do you want to experience in your life-time? Don't dilly-dally and ponder this; answer it in rapid-fire fashion: no logic, don't overanalyze, just write what comes to mind and heart.

Once you've written your response, sit back, look at your list, and compare it to your top five values. Is there a conflict between them, or do they align? Do you feel like you are trying to angle park in a parallel universe?

How Your Values Affect Your Decision Making

By now you are probably wondering why we are spending so much time on our values and the roles we take on. These two parts make up the core programming to what runs your operating system. How do you do your work? With whom do you prefer to spend your time? For whom do you go the extra mile? You have literally been operating either consciously or subconsciously on your core values and have taken on roles that either support your values or, in all likelihood, don't. If you are wondering why some of the roles in life drain you while others energize you, it's truly based on whether that role fits into your top core values or not.

The big task here is to try an experiment for the next few days. Now that you have identified your top five values, I want you to make every one of the decisions that comes your way solely based on whether it falls within your top five values or not. Difficult as it might be for you, you cannot decide to do something that falls outside of your top five values.

For example, a volunteer opportunity comes up and you know it would help you in your upcoming job promotion, but you just listed your top five values as: health, family, spirituality, friendship, and peace. This decision will move you along in your career but will take time away from home, and you won't have as much time to get to the gym. So within your current top five, you would decide not to take on that board position. Living within your values is not always easy. It takes some discipline, but the payoff is huge. You will have a surge of energy and be truly engaged in the activities you decide to take on.

On the other hand, let's say you have been asked to coach your daughter's ball team. Even though you feel swamped at work right now and your yard really needs some solid attention, one of your top five values is to spend quality time with your kids. If you take on the coaching position, you will no doubt spend many hours driving with your daughter to and from the ball diamond, which will give you lots of chat time in the car. And you will be spending several more hours reconnecting with her during games. Work will take you a bit longer, but your decision is then made on what you value, which actually brings you more into a balanced life.

This is a task I want you to try for a few days, but you might want to discontinue after that. Of course, that is entirely up to you, but I would hope that you would continue and reap the wonderful benefits by living in this authentic way.

Chapter Six

WHISTLE WHILE YOU WORK: HOW MUSIC, PLAY, HUMOUR, AND CREATIVITY ENERGIZE AND ENGAGE YOU

Richelle Lawrence

I once read that what counts in life is not the number of hours you put in, but how much of yourself you put into the hours. This certainly resonates with me. How often have you felt as though you really didn't have the energy, enthusiasm, or heart to really engage with the people around you or your work? Have you ever found yourself suddenly at work and weren't quite sure how you got there? Have you spent a busy day "doing" and by the end of the day wondered what you actually "did" the whole day? Have you had a conversation with someone and can't remember what you talked about? Have you gone to tell someone about your weekend and can't remember what happened? I know I definitely have been there!

There are some simple solutions to helping re-energize and re-engage in life that are fun to do and don't involve drudgery. When life is all too serious, it is time to do a "fun audit." Here's how it goes:

When was the last time you…

- Danced or sang to your favourite song?
- Did something you love to do for no reason at all?
- Laughed so hard you cried?
- Put yourself first either at home or at work…just because?
- Said to yourself, "Life doesn't get any better than this?"

- Felt tired and void of energy?
- Felt stressed out and overwhelmed?

My guess is that you can easily recall the feelings of being tired, stressed, and overwhelmed by the everyday challenges. I will also guess that the last time you experienced fun and joy might be a bit tougher for you to remember.

You may think you need to make a few changes, and you're probably right. Filling your life with music, play, humour, and creativity will allow you to:

- refuel and manage the challenges of everyday life;
- re-energize;
- re-engage with the world around you;
- improve your attitude, relationships, and work environment; and
- boost your outlook on your future.

For many of us, it is hard to imagine how these simple things can help us achieve all this, but the use of music, Silly Putty, toys, balloons, bubbles, Lego, paint, chalk, comedy, and just having fun—such as we experienced as kids—can actually:

- increase joy and happiness;
- lower stress and enhance wellness;
- improve attitude and morale;
- enhance creativity;
- strengthen relationships;
- stimulate engagement;
- boost energy levels; and
- help with problem solving.

Unfortunately, as we go from being a kid to taking on the responsibilities that go along with being an adult, we stop playing. Adjusting to a career, starting a family, and managing the busy life of a "grown up" can do this to us, but failing to engage in joyful activities has consequences. Many of us have adopted that "mature adult syndrome" and have completely forgotten how to appreciate music, play, humour, and creativity like we did when we were children. Apart from being self-conscious and not wanting to be viewed as silly, juvenile, or immature, we make excuses such as, "I'm too busy" or "I can't afford it." We all want to *appear* younger, but none of us wants to *act* younger. Is it possible that the two are connected?

Whether at work or at home, incorporating music, play, humour, and creativity into your day-to-day routine is important to a fulfilling life, so let's dive a little deeper into the whys, hows, and dos of having a little more fun in life.

If you think this is a little silly and somewhat of a time waster, I am asking you to indulge me and think outside the box, around the box, in the box, or maybe jump into a new box all together. I want you to actually try something a little fun. Yes...right now.

Boost with Music

Wherever you are, turn up the radio or fire up your iPod and find your favourite song. Now start singing at the top of your lungs! Who cares who's listening or if you can't sing? If you have to close the door, that's fine, but just do it—get singing!

Many studies have been conducted to find the deeper benefits of listening to and playing music. From increased fetal development to the amplification of everyday emotions, there's mounting evidence pointing to music as an improvement to our lives. Music has been shown to have an effect on mood, energy levels, motor skills, pain management, memory, IQ, productivity, and concentration.

Consider how the right song can put you in a better mood and soothe emotional turmoil. There are times when certain songs help us feel energized or calm us, depending on our circumstances. The main reason behind this phenomenon is that music has the ability to verbalize and express our feelings better than any other medium. We have favourite songs for particular situations because we tune into the melodies that capture our vibe the best.

It is helpful to identify songs and music that create relationships between our mood and the music. That way you'll know what song or CD to play to give you the lift or the calm you need in any given moment.

Have you ever noticed how pumped you get when listening to a rocking Bon Jovi song while at the gym or hiking a trail? Now flip your iPod to Enya and take note of how much harder it is to really get moving. It has been suggested that stimulating music can actually increase muscle tension, while sedative music decreases it. This is probably why the aerobics, kickboxing, or spin instructor uses dance music in the background rather than elevator music to get you pumped.

Several studies, including one conducted by Janet Gilbert at Colorado State University on 808 children ages three to six, point overwhelmingly to a correlation between increased motor ability (both large and small) following the introduction of music. Music also has the ability to ease the perception of chronic pain. In fact, according to a paper published in the *Journal of Advanced Nursing*, music can reduce chronic pain by up to twenty-one percent.

Various research has found that playing music in the workplace has positive effects on employees and customers. In 1999, music psychologist Adrian North of the University of Leicester investigated the effects of music within the workplace. The study took place in a data input area of a bank. Over the course of three weeks, staff were exposed to fast, slow, and no music. Productivity was assessed and all staff taking part in the study were asked to complete a questionnaire at the end of each day. The research revealed that:

- Productivity is lower when no music is played.
- Fast music really does improve the productivity levels of employees.
- Playing music results in higher employee morale.

Professor of Music Richard McGregor of the University of Cubria found that playing music at work can increase productivity and lead to a happier and more motivated workforce. He believes the right level of background music can make the day seem shorter, keep spirits high, and reduce the number of stressful situations that can otherwise occur. However, he noted that choosing the wrong type of music can cause office arguments and lead to more problems than it was intended to solve. To avoid these issues, find out what is the most preferred music and turn it on and see how much better you all work and how improved your moods will be.

As long as radios have been around, music has enhanced our lives, both at work and at home. With music, we are more productive and time seems to pass more quickly.

Whether it's mopping the floors or doing the office filing, all the chores seem effortless with a little music.

Boost with Play

My interest in play and my passion to inspire others to play has come from my experiences. As a child, I had the opportunity to experience play in a big way. My parents provided us with chances to participate in sports and the arts. We travelled frequently and went on camping trips in places close to home and abroad. We climbed trees tall enough to see the ocean in the distance, played backyard games of all kinds, spent hours in the park hanging on the monkey bars, built elaborate forts, and fell asleep in warm and cozy sleeping bags while watching for shooting stars under the open sky. Life was filled with fun and joy—at least it was for me and the kids around me!

On the other hand, I watched my mom and dad go to work each day only to come home to cook and clean, chauffer us around to activities and events, and take care of our every need. At the time, it didn't occur to me that my mom, in putting us first, missed out on the fun and joy in life—the *play!*

I think that watching my parents for so many years has somehow made me hypersensitive to whether people are playing in their lives. It has certainly led me to research, read about, and study the benefits of play. It has made me very interested in finding ways to encourage others to have fun and find the joy in their lives.

What images do you conjure up when you think about weekends, holidays, or retirement? Do they all make you think of having fun whenever you want? Do you think about reading a good book, swimming in the ocean, hiking in the mountains, playing golf, gardening, or even sleeping?

For many, time off means having a chance to let go of all the stresses, tasks, and challenges of life for just a little while. For some, it means doing something you have been putting off because you have been too busy, tired, or feeling guilty. Many have plans to try something they have never done before at a point in their lives when they can really focus and put their attention to it. I want you to think about why *play* is not your priority in your life. Why you are waiting until the weekend, for holidays, or your retirement?

Stuart Brown, a physician, psychiatrist, clinical researcher, and founder of the National Institute for Play, studies the nature of people's play experiences over their lifetimes. His studies have revealed that play is significant for both children and adults. He found highly creative and successful individuals tend to have a rich play life. He found that play affects mental and physical health for both adults and children. A severely play-deprived child demonstrates many dysfunctional symptoms—the evidence continues to accumulate that the learning of emotional control, social competency, personal resiliency, and continuing curiosity, as well as other life benefits, accrue largely through rich developmentally appropriate play experiences. Like children, adults who have lost what was a playful youth and don't play will demonstrate social, emotional, and cognitive narrowing; be less able to handle stress; and often experience depression. His conclusion is that play is who we are.

Playing and having fun actually keep you healthy. If you are a busy working person, a parent, a caregiver of family members, or someone who is just trying to keep up with the pace of life, finding time to play is sometimes difficult. Although it can be challenging to find time to play, your life depends on it. The formula is simple: Play + Fun = Laughter. This will result in reduced stress, increased oxygen to your body, decreased risk of hypertension and depression, improved immunity, stronger relationships, and much more.

I realize that many have already figured out how to include play in their lives on a daily or at least a weekly basis. I encourage you to share your success and model it for others. However, if you are still missing play in your life, give these questions some thought:

- When was the last time you did something for the pure joy of it?
- When was the last time you got down and dirty with your kids, grandkids, or other people's kids and really played with them?
- When was the last time you played a game with family or friends?
- When was the last time you simply did *something fun?*

Ask yourself, "What do I consider play? What gets in my way of playing more? What's taking its place?" The definition of play is different for all of us. It's not something easily defined. However, some say that play is a state of mind, a state of body, an emotion, and a part of our spirit. It is something you do (playing games, swinging, playing sports), but it is also something you enjoy watching others do. People often describe it as a time when we feel most alive. Play is one of those things that we just take for granted when we're young but evidently jettison as we get older. It's as natural to a healthy balanced life as breathing. It's not just for kids!

When I think of play, it's something that brings me joy, makes me laugh, helps me forget about the things going on in my life, and lifts my spirits. To you, play might include watching sports; for others, it might be participating in them. For you, it could be participating in a theatrical performance; for others, it's being in the audience. Whatever play is for you, it's time to include more of it in your life. Below are some ideas to help you figure out how to begin playing.

First, explore your interest in current hobbies that fall into the following four categories:

1. **Collecting hobbies** (coins, baseball cards, miniatures, buttons, snowmen)
2. **Crafting hobbies** (woodworking, quilting, baking, crafts, painting)
3. **Doing hobbies** (skating, playing the guitar, golfing, fishing, walking, working out, playing chess)
4. **Learning hobbies** (reading, travelling, watching the Discovery Channel)

Second, look at the basic needs we all have and see if your play meets these needs:

1. **Social needs.** As humans, we need a certain amount of interaction with others.
2. **Physical needs.** Locomotion is a requirement for good health.
3. **Expressive needs.** We have a need to express ourselves through music, art, poetry, baking, writing, etc.

4. **Intellectual needs.** We have a need to learn and grow throughout our lives. Keeping the mind alert can slow of the progression of dementia or Alzheimer's disease.

Third, look at who you include with your play:

1. **Individual play** (reading, cooking, walking)
2. **Leisure partner** (movies, plays, concerts, hikes, dinner out, vacations)
3. **Family play** (parents, children, grandparents, siblings)
4. **Friends** (socials, spectator sports, cookouts)

So how much fun are you really having? How are you playing, both at home and at work? I want you to spend some time doing the following:

- Make a list of your favourite fun things to do, and get doing at least two of them!
- Dust off an old board game and play with your family or friends.
- Kick off your shoes, turn up the tunes, and dance.
- Schedule a play date! Schedule some time to have fun with friends.
- Organize a picnic.
- Stop at a park and get on that swing set. How high can you reach?
- Go for a hike. Pay attention to the beauty around you. Feel your heartbeat.
- Play a game of urban golf. This is something I plan to do in the near future. The idea is golf in the city streets. Now, if you are like my husband, you are thinking this

is a bit nuts. I have looked into it and I think it would be so much fun. I have to figure out what kind of balls to use and how to get around the traffic, but when I do, look out world!

I have facilitated many workshops and sessions on play, and it is always interesting how many people comment on how they really want to play more. I recently participated in a retreat with over twenty women who created a vision board (a collage of pictures representing their goals for the future). Every one of them indicated a desire to include more play in their lives, and it piqued my interest in creating more play opportunities for women.

Over the last few months, I have spent some time trying to organize play-filled activities called Play Parties for Gal Pals. As the number of participants grew from twelve to fifty in just three months, I am again reminded at how important play is for people.

Play is not just for outside the workplace. It is something that can enhance the energy and engagement level of employees, their managers, and their customers. It only makes sense that teams of people who play together really get to know one another. When you know more about the people in your workplace, it becomes easier to communicate, solve problems, and creatively manage both good and difficult situations.

Unfortunately, many CEOs view work and play as being mutually exclusive; however, experience shows that play-based companies have the potential of being transformative, allowing its people to be innovative problem solvers, creating new possibilities and reaching higher limits. Play helps our brains become smarter and adaptable, both of which help all of us be more effective and engaged at work.

There are, however, an increasing number of CEOs who understand the benefits of play and having fun in the workplace. Some have even developed a vision statement to address the importance of play and have employees and customers engage in play on a daily basis. I once had a career opportunity with WestJet Airlines. They were seeking an individual to direct the 737 Fun Club. That's right! They were actually looking for a person to organize the fun activities and events for their employees and their families. Now *that* is dedication to play!

If you need to have a little more fun and play at work, consider the following:

- Find a joke book to share with someone at work.
- Play some music.
- Play an appropriate practical joke on a colleague.
- Bring in ice cream and cones for everyone.
- Try a game of office mini golf. All you need are putters, waste baskets, and whatever obstacles you can create.
- Turn a meeting into a fun activity. Try a scavenger hunt that teaches more about the workplace; a riddle worksheet to address new concepts; or an "Amazing Race" or "Survivor Challenge" for team building.
- Organize staff recognition gatherings (BBQ, potlucks, volunteer day).
- Smile for no reason!

When you are engaged and energized through play activities at home and work, you are more productive, creative, innovative, and dedicated to whatever it is you are trying to achieve.

Boost with Humour

As they say, "laughter is the best medicine!" Humour and the laughter that comes with it are truly beneficial to your mind and body. Both strengthen your immune system, boost your energy, diminish pain, and protect you from the damaging effects of stress. Best of all, this priceless medicine is fun, free, and easy to use.

There is something attractive about a humorous person, isn't there? Their laughter is contagious and their energy is infectious. They inspire the people around them and make them more light-hearted. Being around someone with a great sense of humour and cheerful laughter can actually lift your spirits to a point where you forget your pain, your challenges, and your stress.

Whether you are at home or at work, humour can keep you emotionally healthy. When we find humour and can laugh at ourselves, we can strengthen our relationships with our partners, children, co-workers, bosses, and customers. We can harness it to buffer against disagreements and disappointments.

Some of the easy ways to incorporate humour and laughter into your life include:

- watching a funny movie or TV show;
- reading a funny story or joke book;
- going to a comedy club;
- seeking out funny people;
- playing with a pet (my boxer Champ always makes me

laugh); and

- attending a laughter yoga class.

Boost with Creativity

Traits of creativity, such as curiosity, playfulness, and the need to experiment and try new things, come to children as easily as breathing. They're simply second nature. However, as we age, like play, many of us experience a diminishing creativity. It's never too late, however, to turn things around. Being creative makes us happier and healthier, and it re-energizes us and re-engages us to the world.

Creativity can help us think about life in new ways. It helps us evaluate questions about what we want, what comes next, how to foster change, and how to enhance our well-being. Creativity can help us find meaning and purpose as we move through life and grow older.

John Mirowsky, a sociology professor at the Population Research Center of the University of Texas at Austin, found that "creative activity is non-routine, enjoyable, and provides opportunity for learning and for solving problems. People who do creative work, whether paid or not, feel healthier and have fewer physical problems." When people make an effort to be creative in their workplace, they are more likely to be stable in their job, take fewer sick days, and work with a positive attitude. When people are in positions where their job is routine such as an assembly line, it is important that they try to switch things up. This might mean changing positions on the line or finding something creative to do at break times. Simple additions of creativity in a workplace can help people find more joy in their work. When we do creative work or creative activities, we improve our ability to solve problems and we strengthen our immune systems with the endorphins released during the experiences.

The Town Planning Network's 1999 research highlighted the importance of developing a creative mindset, a concept that is relevant for initial professional education, practice, and continuing professional development alike. Creative thinking is a key capability that helps individuals and organizations deal with and manage change, which is fundamental to the nature of life and business today.

Walt Disney is a great example of a creative person. He used his unique ideas to bring to life an amazing media and entertainment empire for children and adults alike. Through his imagination and creativity, he developed opportunities and experiences for all of us to enjoy. It's difficult to avoid experiencing some creativity and stretching your imagination when you enter into one of Disney's theme parks, even if this means simply conjuring up thoughts of how someone could have actually taken these ideas and made them a reality.

When interviewing potential candidates for employment, some companies have them participate in hands-on creative experiences. These companies realize that creative employees are valuable and tend to be successful, in turn making the company successful. They also find that those who struggle with creativity struggle with their work.

To reintroduce yourself to being creative, you must commit to the following:

1. Believe creativity is important to you both personally and professionally.
2. Experiment with being creative by trying something new.

3. Be creative at least once a week.

Some Ideas on How to Boost Your Creativity

Listen to music. Try to listen to genres different from what you normally listen to.

Brainstorm. Brainstorming can help you come up with tons of new ideas in addition to deciding which is best. Hold an intentional conversation. There is a new movement called World Café, where you get creative with your ideas through conversations rather than from building lists.

Always carry a small notebook and pen with you. Whenever you are struck with an idea, you should always be in a position to write it down no matter where you are or what you are doing. Upon reviewing your notes, you may discover that around ninety percent of your ideas are daft. Don't worry; that's normal. What's important is that about ten percent are brilliant.

- **Take an art class.** The type of art doesn't matter: writing, visual, music, acting, etc. Just try something different. It's okay to feel awkward.

- **Define your problem.** Grab a sheet of paper, smartphone, computer, or whatever you use to make notes, and define your problem in detail. You'll probably find ideas positively spewing out once you've done this.

- **If you can't think, go for a walk.** A change of atmosphere is good for you, and gentle exercise helps shake up the brain cells. Spend some energy and let your mind wander while you move.

- **Don't watch TV.** Few things in the world will zap your creativity more than the ubiquitous boob tube.

- **Read as much as you can and as widely as you can.** Books exercise your brain, provide inspiration, and fill you with information that allows you to easily make creative connections.

- **Exercise your brain.** Brains, like bodies, need exercise to keep fit. If you don't exercise your brain, it will get flabby and useless. Exercise your brain by reading, speaking with clever people, and disagreeing with people—arguing can be a terrific way to give your brain cells a workout.

Life brings with it challenges and hurdles that can either get the best of you or help you grow and become more than you were the day before. When you include music, play, humour, and creativity in your life, managing the obstacles becomes much easier. As fun becomes a part of your everyday life, both at work and at home, you will feel more energized and engaged. Your ability to be creative, find more balance, see the positive in life, solve problems, and strengthen relationships will become second nature.

From this point forward, listen to the music, play more, laugh a lot, and be creative. Whistle while you work.

Chapter Seven

Contribution: How Giving Back Creates Better People, Better Teams, and Stronger Bottom Lines

This is where we give back for no other reason than it's just simply the right thing to do. The idea of philanthrocapitalism has had such a groundswell over the past couple of years, and consumers are keen to work with and buy from companies that are doing as much for the world as they are for their shareholders. It is no longer solely the responsibility of our governments to make things right in the world. Besides, the rest of us can usually get things done much quicker and more cost effectively than large governmental departments. Your team or family need to choose a cause you can all get behind and get to it.

My suggestion is to choose one to take on every week. If you find that this interferes with the flow of things, try going to once a month for six months. However, I caution you not to let it drop to anything less frequent than once a month. I also recommend that it continue for no less than six months.

What can you expect to see by implementing this new way of doing business?

- More collaboration
- More focus
- Improved communication
- Better productivity
- More work in fewer hours
- Less "I" and more "we" in the communication

At this point you may be asking, "How, if I add one more thing to my team's already full plate, are we going to achieve all of this?" The answer is simple. Part of why we are unproductive is because we are stuck in the old ways of doing things. Whether it's taking on too much "stuff," not effectively communicating our needs, not hearing what our team members have to say, or (here's the biggie) multitasking, we're effectively doing a half-assed job of everything.

We've already addressed most of these, and now we're going address the art of multitasking. We often tell ourselves that we can do multiple things simultaneously. This is nonsense. Perhaps you can walk and chew gum at the same time, but how often have you been on the phone with someone while you were typing an e-mail? How many mistakes did you have to go back and correct and how often did you have to ask the person to repeat themselves?

These are seemingly simple tasks. Try being in a meeting and collaborating while texting someone. There's a reason why I suggest all PDAs go into a basket at the beginning of every meeting. Humans are terrible at multitasking. We say we can do it, but clearly we cannot.

When implementing this new way of doing things, it may initially seem like your team has added one more thing to its plate, but in reality two things will happen:

1. Your team will look forward to it.
2. They'll prioritize their work day to fit it in.

What are some of the things that your team and you can do that gives back to the community and is about team building? Below are some suggestions.

Build a House for a Homeless Family

For years, Habitat for Humanity has been offering corporate volunteering opportunities for team-building events. Think of how many people are homeless in your area. Rather than write a cheque, which is what most of us do, help build a family a house that they'll have for years to come. If you think about that cheque that you wrote, generous thought it may be, it only helped feed that family for a day, maybe a week. When basic needs such as housing are met, we have a clearer mind to get a job, to feed our families, and to sleep. Think how well you sleep in your own bed every night. For you, this is a necessity, for some, sadly, it's a luxury.

While you won't build an entire house in one day, you will get messy—building trenches, putting up insulation, installing wall sockets, maybe doing some drywalling, and certainly painting and things like that. They have contractors for laying foundations and adding a roof, windows, doors, etc., but your contributions will be immesurable!

Literacy Volunteers

I have a friend who's been volunteering two days a month to go to the public school near his place of employment to teach kids how to read for four hours. Some of these kids have special needs and reading is a challenge for them. Others were slow to develop because their mothers did drugs during their pregnancy and their phsyical challenges kept them from being able to focus and so they fell behind. Still others are learning English as their second language and need a little help to avoid falling too far behind in school.

Initially, my friend did this on his own. While the company "sanctioned" it and paid him for his service time, this was not part of any organized team building. After five years of doing this, his company asked him to head up the literacy volunteer program and now scores of his co-workers volunteer at several schools in the city.

Make-A-Wish Foundation

You may not be old enough to remember this, but Babe Ruth, the famous New York Yankees slugger, fulfilled one dying child's wish by visiting him in the hospital. A visit from "The Babe" was all this young boy wanted,

Imagine how often kids are left in hospitals with few relatives visiting them. Perhaps their parents must work round the clock to pay for their child's medical care. A visit from anyone means so much in the life of a terminally ill patient, especially a child.

The Make-A-Wish Foundation doesn't just grant people hospital visits. They also take a dying patient to a baseball game or to a concert that he or she would otherwise not see. Maybe a ten-year-old's dying wish is to see Stevie Wonder in concert. Make-A-Wish makes it happen; they just need people to help make it happen. That's where you come in. Do something for your local Children's Hospital.

Offer Career Advice to Teens at Risk

Volunteering with kids at risk is becoming more popular and so there are growing opportunities for help. What better service to offer than career advice to inmates anticipating parole? Imagine how much life experience and advice you have to offer. Help them get a leg up and give them reasons to avoid poor and even bad choices. When they're more productive, they have the same sense of pride that any of us has for doing a good job.

What can you offer this program? Well, that's almost too easy to answer. There are a million reasons to go back and get a high school diploma or equivilency and go to college. You can help kids study for their upcoming equivilency exam. If they've gotten a degree or diploma, you can help them study to get their master's. Encourage them to pursue what makes them happy and will make them more fulfilled. The same advice you would offer them is what you'd tell your own kids or nieces and nephews.

Local SPCA and City-Run Animal Shelters

Who can turn down an opportunity to cuddle with a puppy or a kitten? Maybe that ten-year-old cat that a family recently gave up because it was clawing the furniture just needs a little love. If only these animals could talk, they'd probably tell you some horrible stories. All they really need is a little love. In the case of dogs, some training is required so that when a family comes to meet them, they're not turned off by bad behaviour, which helps them find homes.

But shelters don't just want people to cuddle; they also need volunteers to clean the crates, take dogs for walks, administer medicine, change dressing on wounds, clean out ears, you name it!

Helping socialize an animal that may have been on the fringe of becoming feral can save his or her life.

Build a Community Garden

We tend to take for granted how our yards look. Whether we do it ourselves or pay someone to come in, we at least have some plants, probably flowers, and maybe even a couple of trees to brighten our day at home. If you're anything like me, your yard is a sanctuary away from the everyday. But imagine living in an urban area in the inner city, especially where you're surrounded by nothing but concrete, asphalt, and buildings. High-rises are filled with people who may have never seen a garden. If you and I love ours, why can't they love one too?

The vacant lot across the street from your office might be a perfect spot to create a community garden. You have the tools in your garage already. Between all the members of your team, surely you have all the dirt, the diggers, the spades, the shovels, and the trowels necessary to plant some flowers.

The first visit you can all amend the soil, which, as you know, will take a bit of effort. On the next visit, start planting. You could plant fruits and vegetables, as poor families tend to lack access to fresh healthy food. Maybe one of you had plans to remove a tree in your backyard that was in the way of your kids' future swing set. Transplant it to the community garden. In a few years time, it will grow to be something the kids can climb, or just sit under to shade them from the sun and filter out some of the noise their lives take in on a daily basis. You never know what joy you are going to bring to a few kids or a few families.

Perhaps by your second visit you will have volunteers from the neighbourhood wishing to help you and ask you questions. The more volunteers you have, the better the likelihood that after your volunteering is over, they'll maintain the garden for you. As with anything, when people feel included, they're far more likely to contribute, maintain, and come up with ideas. It's no different than your team at work.

On your future visits, you can bring more flowers. Maybe you can get together some wood to make a bench for the locals to sit on and read or just dream about what life could be like outside of their everyday surroundings.

One thing is for certain: the garden your team helps create will serve as an important part of the neighbourhood, and people will not only protect it, but cherish it.

Be a Day Camp Counsellor

Contrary to what you might think, camp counselling is not just for teenagers. While it's probably true that teenagers often jump at the opportunity to leave home for five weeks in the summer and would prefer to deal with a bunch of kids rather than their own parents, day camp is different—most of the counsellors are adults.

Whether you volunteer to teach or build a volcano, it doesn't really matter much. You'll love the interaction and so will the kids. It's simply a win-win for everyone.

Some kids go to day camp because Mom and Dad simply can't look after them all day while they work. Sound familiar? Some go as a way to stay out of trouble. Whatever the reasons are, kids crave structure and adult mentoring. Maybe you'll be fortunate and be able to volunteer on a day when they have an outing to a local park or a tourist attraction and you'll really be able to put your teaching skills to use.

You may not know it at the time, but volunteering as a day camp counsellor may help a child stay on the good side of the law. You have no idea what you say or do that can have a lasting impression on someone whose path you never crossed and whose home life you're unaware of. As a past camp counsellor myself, I guarantee you that you will never have as good a night's sleep as you will after a day spent with a couple dozen kids.

Juvenile Detention Centres

You can make a huge difference on kids and catch them before they go on to a life of crime. Introduce them to the positive and rewarding alternatives before someone else exposes them to more of what they've already had a taste of. Don't underestimate your ability to influence a young mind to choose a direction other than the one in which they were headed.

Juvenile detention centres house teenagers from thirteen to eighteen. You know from your kids or nieces and nephews how impressionable this age bracket can be. Encourage them to finish school and show them what a life without crime can be like, what they can achieve with a little determination and hard work. The kids in these centres are mostly serving sentences for petty crimes and therefore any criminal record will be expunged once they're released. Give them that fresh start they so desparately need.

Bring in college applications and show them what they could be studying. You might be surprised the difference you can make. And on top of that, this sort of thing can have a snowball effect. They'll go home and try and prevent their younger siblings from following in their footsteps and encourage them to make different and more positive choices. Through your one-on-one volunteer work, you could influence more than just the one life without realizing it.

Adopt-A-Family

Organizations all over the U.S. and Canada are popping up that allow people to adopt a family and help them with their basic necessities. We tend to think of this as being an issue during the holidays when we are opening presents either for

Christmas or Chanukah. We are reminded then that there are many children who won't be opening any presents at all, and the needs for these families go well beyond the holidays. In all likelihood, they've gone without eating a few times and their kids' clothes are tattered and torn.

Now, this gets tricky because we again have this tendancy to pull out our chequebooks. This is not the best solution. While they indeed have some immediate needs, they also require some skills that will help them in the future. Help a family learn different skills that they can use for weeks, months, and even years from now. Teach them about proper nutrition; teach them how to balance their chequebooks; maybe Mom or Dad is illiterate.

Serve up lunches at the local community shelter. Take lunches to shut-in seniors. Help a school in a developing country. Sort food at the food bank after you have done a good food drive.

Hold a "Just Be-Cause" Event

I encourage you to hold a Just Be-Cause fundraiser to help girls in Nepal get out of slavery and into school. I raise funds to buyout young girls in Nepal from bonded contract labour situations so that they can attend school. If this is something your team would be interested in doing, then I encourage you to host one of these events. I import scarves from Nepal and sell them when I speak. I use the money raised to buyout these contracts and pay for the girls to go to school. It's easy and the money goes a long way. Go to www.iwencanada.com to find out more about the charity and how you can help.

Any one of these activities will allow your team to think outside of themselves. You will find that they'll start thinking of days ahead of time, putting together plans to implement for their next trip and looking forward to carrying out those plans. Going from self-centred to selfless is possible for all of us, regardless of our politics, religion, personality, and upbringing.

Whatever you decide to do, as a team it's important that you decide for yourself. There are many other volunteer programs that I didn't list, but a simple Google search will reveal others. These are just some of the many that I know have been tried and tested.

If you try this with your family and are successful, apply the principles to your team at work, and vice versa. Your kids will learn the value of thinking of others before themselves and you never know what influence this may have on them and their future.

It seems an appropriate time to conclude not only my book but also the story of Jake and Tessa. I thank you for taking the time to read both. I hope you have learned something and that your team will be a better functioning and cohesive group. If I have achieved only that, I will be happy. However, I also hope that you continue to implement cellular-free Fridays and decide to become cellular free always when you are driving.

Cheers,

Linda

Three Quarters of the Way to Love cont.

For months they'd been carrying on this illicit affair—stealing glances, meeting in the janitor's closet, and once even on the roof. The excitement was something he'd surely never experienced, but this made no sense to Jake. Was Tessa some kind of split personality?

Over time, Jake realized that Tessa did nothing half way, including sex. It finally dawned on him that this was Tessa and he was in love! She actually was quite consistent with everything she did, almost to a fault.

"For months I have been seeing Tessa and carrying on an affair with her. We met on the subway. Coincidentally, both of us were on our way here to interview for the same position. I was initially attracted to her for her looks, which are stunning, don't you agree?"

Before anyone could answer, Jake continued, "But I saw beyond that immediately and saw a strong-willed, practical, intelligent, driven woman with a streak in her that I knew I had to get to know better.

"Regardless whether both or neither of us had gotten hired, I was going to ask this woman out. Women like Tessa don't come around very often. You know that, and I know that even better!

"We had our first date, and from that moment on we were inseparable. I couldn't wait to be with her at the end of each day. I am so surprised none of you picked up on the feelings that were being transmitted through the air. I know many of you are probably shocked because I have said more in the last three minutes than I have said to anyone in the last three years. I am not exactly a talkative guy. Indeed, Tessa pokes fun at me because she says that I am a Neanderthal. Okay,

it's deserved.

"About two weeks ago, Tessa did something that made me know for certain that she was the one for me. We were at the park and a man collapsed from what appeared to be a heart attack. I was taking a nap, lying on her lap. Within seconds, my head hit the bench we'd been on, as Tessa, without hesitation, ran over and gave the gentleman mouth-to-mouth resuscitation. I was rudely awakened by my head hitting the bench. I looked up and there she was over top of this man, who was perhaps in his sixties. She was alternating between mouth-to-mouth and chest compressions.

"I found myself in awe of her split-second decision. She didn't hesitate to help that man. Me? I would have hemmed and hawed for ten minutes. I would have weighed the consequences of whether the family would sue me, whether I'd catch a disease, whether people would see me and wonder what was wrong with me. By the time I would have reasoned with myself that it is the right thing to do, the man would have been dead! Tessa, however, never thought of the consequences. This man was dying and needed her help. I am not sure whether she asked for permission of his family or not. Knowing her, she pulled out a contract already drawn up and had them read and sign. Now time is of the essence, she would have reasoned.

"It was at this moment that I realized that this is how Tessa operates. She rarely allows reasonable judgement to stand in her way of doing what is the right thing to do. Oddly, I have concluded that she and I arrive at the same decision ninety-nine percent of the time. However, I am four days behind her because I have analyzed everything at every single angle and weighed options and considered alternatives, while

Tessa has already made up her mind. I often ask myself how we ended up making the same decision, out loud even!"

Jake suddenly walked over to Tessa, who was still on the opposite side of the oval table, knelt down on the floor of the conference room, pulled out a little box, and asked her to marry him!

Everyone in the room was flabbergasted, especially Tessa, but evidently there was also an audience of people peering through the glass. This was the lone conference room in the company, and so it was like a fishbowl. A crowd was gathering all around the outside of the conference room. Jake seemed oblivious to the taps on the glass, the yelling for more onlookers, and to the reactions of everyone in the conference room.

Their boss, John, just stood there with his hand over his mouth. He finally spoke, "I'd say that this was a huge accomplishment for Jake and Tessa, wouldn't you? Not only were they adept at keeping this a secret, but they also have proven something else. Analyzers can work very well with socializers! And thank God he didn't propose with a text message!" The room broke out into laughter, and suddenly every one was hugging one another, especially Jake and Tessa.

References

Brown, Stuart. *Play: How It Shapes the Brain, Opens the Imagination, and Invigorates the Soul*, Avery, 2009.

"Building High Performance Team Culture: Leaving a Lasting Legacy," BreakThroughs, Inc., http://breakthroughsinc.com/what-we-do-team-building.php#teambuilding-culture, accessed 2 July 2010.

Cook, Patricia. "Five Benefits of Cleaning Up Clutter," Associated Content, 19 October 2009, http://www.associatedcontent.com/article/2303229/five_benefits_of_cleaning_up_clutter.html?cat=6.

"Creative thinking in planning: How do we climb outside the box?" *Town Planning Review* 77(2), Liverpool University Press, May 2006: 221–244.

Dwornick, Lorie. "Chemical Warfare Agents And Toxic Waste Disguised As Household Cleaning Products," 18 January 2002, Healthycleaning.ca, http://www.healthycleaning.ca/toxic_facts/chemical_warfare.html.

Gilbert, Jane. "An assessment of motor music skill development in children," *Journal of Research in Music Education* 28(3), Autumn 1980: 167–175.

Leibow, Cathy. "Laughter is the best medicine – and productivity booster," *Employee Benefit News*, 1 March 2010, http://ebn.benefitnews.com/news/laughter-is-the-best-medicine-and-productivity-booster-2683028-1.html.

McGregor, Richard. "Playing music at work is good for you," University of Cumbria, 7 January 2008, http://www.cumbria.ac.uk/AboutUs/News/Research%20News/music%20at%20work.aspx.

Mirowky, John. "Creative Work Has Health Advantages, Population Research Center Study Shows," The University of Texas at Austin, 17 December 2007, http://www.utexas.edu/news/2007/12/17/sociology_creative/.

North, Adrian, and David J. Hargreaves and Jennifer McKendrick. "The effects of music on atmosphere in a bank and a bar," *Journal of Applied Social Psychology* 30(7): 1504–1522.

Sidliecki, Sandra L., and Marion Good. "The effect of music on power, pain, depression and disability," *Journal of Advanced Nursing*, June 2006, 54(5): 553–562.

"The Office of the Future Isn't Paperless. It's Wireless. And It's Wherever You Are," Ipsos North America, 19 December 2006, http://www.ipsos-na.com/news-polls/pressrelease.aspx?id=3312.

www.peterwalshdesign.com

About Linda

Best-Selling Author, Award-Winning Speaker,
Certified Speaking Professional (CSP), Humorist,
"Life Accountability and Perspective Specialist"

Linda Edgecombe, CSP, is an internationally renowned, award-winning, and humorous speaker, trainer, and consultant. She is a best-selling author who energizes every room as she leads people to loosen up, lighten the load, and laugh. Her audiences are motivated and shown how they can shift their perspectives on life, work, and themselves. Change has never been this painless!

As a professional with a degree in physical education, Linda brings 20+ years of recreation, employee wellness, lifestyle, and corporate consulting experience to her programs and her clients. She was a consultant for ParticipACTION, promoting healthy living to Canadians, and is known for being one of the country's most popular speakers. She was most recently featured in the *Wall Street Journal* as an expert in "Shifting Perspectives."

Inside all the laughter, Linda's audiences are inspired to find the meaning in what they do and let go of what's not working. Her message is a welcome as a deep belly laugh and as profound as an honest look in the mirror.

You can find out more about booking Linda at:

Learning Edge Resources
"Accountability with an Edge"
www.lindaedgecombe.com
info@lindaedgecombe.com
1-888-868-9601 or 1-250-868-9601